GUIDEBOOK FOR DEPLOYING DISTRIBUTED RENEWABLE ENERGY SYSTEMS

A CASE STUDY ON THE COBRADOR HYBRID SOLAR PV MINI-GRID

AUGUST 2019

ADB

ASIAN DEVELOPMENT BANK

Contents

Tables, Figures, and Boxes

Tables

Figures

Boxes

Acknowledgments

The *Guidebook for Deploying Distributed Renewable Energy Systems* is an output of a comprehensive study carried out by the Sustainable Development and Climate Change Department (SDCC) of the Asian Development Bank (ADB) under regional technical assistance 8953: Promoting Sustainable Energy for All in Asia and the Pacific - Sustainable Energy for All Regional Hub for Asia and the Pacific (Subproject C). The study was conducted by a team in the Sector Advisory Service Cluster–Energy Sector Group (SDSC-ENE) led by Kee-Yung Nam, principal energy economist. Yongping Zhai, chief of the Energy Sector Group and Robert Guild, chief sector officer of the SDCC provided overall guidance. A group of international and national experts provided invaluable contributions as authors of background papers.

This guidebook was written by a team of experts from the SDSC-ENE, under the guidance of Kee-Yung Nam and the supervision of Yongping Zhai. The team comprised Susumu Yoneoka, energy specialist; Yun Ji Suh, energy specialist; Felicisima Arriola; Elmar Elbling; Lyndree Malang; Charles Cole Navarro; Seoung-Ha Shin; Ana Maria Tolentino; Maria Fritzie Vergel; and Grace Yeneza. Charity Torregosa, senior energy officer; Maria Dona Aliboso, operations analyst; and Angelica Apilado, operations assistant provided technical advisory and administrative support. Ma. Theresa Mercado copyedited the report, and Kris Guico did the layout.

The guidebook benefited from insights and comments of ADB colleagues from the energy divisions of ADB's regional departments. The views and opinions expressed here are those of the authors and do not necessarily reflect those of ADB, its governors, or the governments they represent. The publication of this guidebook is funded by the Asian Clean Energy Fund under the Clean Energy Financing Partnership Facility.

Abbreviations

AC	alternating current
ADB	Asian Development Bank
CO_2	carbon dioxide
DC	direct current
DRES	distributed renewable energy systems
EC	electric cooperative
EPC	engineering procurement and construction
EPIRA	Electric Power Industry Reform Act
ESS	energy storage system
GHG	greenhouse gas
GPS	Global Positioning System
HOMER	Hybrid Optimization of Multiple Energy Resources
KEA	Korea Energy Agency
LCOE	levelized cost of electricity
NEA	National Electrification Administration
NPC–SPUG	National Power Corporation's Small Power Utilities Group
NPP	new power producer
NREL	National Renewable Energy Laboratory
PEP	Philippine Energy Plan
PV	photovoltaic
QTP	qualified third party
RA	Republic Act
ROMELCO	Romblon Electric Cooperative
SHS	solar home system
SPUG	Special Power Utilities Group
UCME	Universal Charge for Missionary Electrification

Weights and Measures

kg	kilogram
km	kilometer
kWh	kilowatt-hour
kW	kilowatt
m^2	square meter
MW	megawatt

Executive Summary

Ensuring affordable, reliable, sustainable, and modern energy for all that meets environmental goals has become central to development and energy policy making. The Sustainable Development Goals 7 and 13 under the 2030 Agenda for Sustainable Development, and the Nationally Determined Contributions under the Paris Agreement advocate universal energy access that mitigates climate change. Transforming development trajectories on a course toward sustainable development entails adopting more renewable resources in providing modern energy for all.

The developing countries of the Asia and Pacific region have been progressing well in providing modern energy—in particular electricity—but rural and remote areas lag behind. According to the International Energy Agency (2018), over 900 million people have gained access to electricity in developing economies in Asia from 2000 to 2017. However, about 351 million still don't have electricity access in 2017, the majority of whom are in rural areas.

Grid extension has been effective in bringing the region's electrification rates to current levels. However, it is not financially and economically viable in remote and isolated rural areas. Geographic complexity, remoteness, and low electricity demand make extending transmission and distribution too costly. However, the use of distributed renewable energy systems (DRES) presents an alternative solution. The use of DRES could be temporary or permanent. It could complement and supplement national electrification plans, and support the universal access and climate change mitigation goals of the region's developing countries.

Pursuing DRES solutions entails an enabling legal, regulatory, and market environment, an understanding of locally available natural resources given the electricity demand, and the ability to choose the optimal renewable energy technology or combination of technologies. The Asian Development Bank, through its Energy for All Initiative—also known as Energy for All—has been providing its developing member countries with technical assistance to increase lending activities in energy access, and assist in formulating energy strategies that fulfill the Sustainable Development Goals and the developing member countries' respective Nationally Determined Contributions. Experience through the years consequently developed into a framework—comprising regulatory, institutional, and market scanning; supply and demand analysis; project design optimization; project implementation; and social, economic, and environmental impact assessment—that could guide the deployment of DRES in remote and isolated rural areas.

Of primary importance is scanning the legal, regulatory, and market environment, which influences the feasibility and growth potential of DRES. Often, remote and isolated rural areas are not commercially viable, which necessitates government support and intervention. The World Bank's *Regulatory Indicators for Sustainable Energy* suggests looking into a national electrification program and legal framework for distributed electrification, the ability to charge cost-reflective tariffs, and the provision of financial incentives.

Executive Summary

Understanding the electricity needs and renewable energy potential of an area is essential for a sound electrification plan. This will help a country determine which remote and isolated areas need government support to increase the viability of adopting DRES. This would also help determine an area's available renewable resources that could be tapped for DRES. The geospatial mapping provides an overview of the distributed and off-grid markets of a country, and reconciles the data sets on energy supply and demand on national and specific areas. To further understand an area's electricity requirements, the Multi-Tier Framework organizes the levels of access in terms of electricity supply, services, and consumption, and can help select possible renewable energy technologies depending on the characteristics of the site.

The renewable resources, electricity requirements, and available renewable energy technologies in the area determine the renewable energy technology or combination of technologies to be used. With so much to consider, optimization tools, such as the Hybrid Optimization of Multiple Energy Resources, can help analyze the performance and cost of an electrification system, and suggest the least-cost technology options. Conducting a social, economic, and environmental impact assessment is recommended after deploying DRES to assess and quantify the benefits to the community. Documenting both the quantitative and qualitative benefits will be valuable for future replication.

With the Philippine government's support, the framework had been applied to Cobrador Island's hybrid solar photovoltaic mini-grid. The pilot project extended the island's electricity access from 8 hours to 24 hours a day, which resulted in increased entrepreneurial activities; more and better livelihood opportunities and tourism potential; enhanced social services (healthcare, education, and security and safety); and more environmentally conscious residents. Other benefits include an increase in the number of grid-connected households from 161 to 260, a lower tariff from ₱30 ($0.60) to ₱15 ($0.30) per kilowatt-hour, and a potential reduction of carbon dioxide emissions by 52,600 kilograms per year from 2015 to 2017. The Cobrador case demonstrates the importance of government support, an enabling legal and regulatory environment, accurate and realistic demand estimates, and building local capacity for operation and maintenance.

With energy policymakers, development investors, and other stakeholders as intended audience, this report aims to offer guidelines for incorporating distributed electrification in national electrification programs, present techniques and tools that can be used to optimize utilization of renewable energy sources for off-grid electrification, present the case study of the Philippines' Cobrador Island solar photovoltaic-diesel hybrid mini-grid, and document the outcomes and lessons to contribute in mainstreaming DRES solutions.

1 Introduction

Energy has long been regarded as a source of economic growth and social development. In recent years, energy policy making has evolved to include environmental goals. It received special focus in 2015, when the United Nations declared energy as part of the 2030 Agenda for Sustainable Development advocating the provision of affordable, reliable, sustainable, and modern energy for all under Sustainable Development Goal (SDG) 7. Energy also figures in the other SDG goals but more prominently in SDG 13, which promotes urgent action to combat climate change and its impacts. In relation, the Paris Climate Agreement contracts countries to fulfill their Nationally Determined Contributions of reducing emissions and adapting to climate change impacts. Indeed, shifting development trajectories to a sustainable development course has become the norm, and would entail adopting more renewable resources in the provision of modern energy for all.

Access to modern energy, in particular electricity, has been a precursor to better livelihood and living conditions, and a necessary requirement for poverty reduction. According to the International Energy Agency (IEA), over 900 million people have gained access to electricity in developing economies in Asia from 2000 to 2017, with electricity access growing from 67% to 91% of the region's total population on the said period (IEA 2018). Notable contributors to this milestone are the People's Republic of China, which achieved universal electricity access last 2015; India, which has given half a billion people basic electricity access since 2000; Bangladesh, which has seen an average of 8% annual increases in electricity access rates over the last 7 years to 2017; and Bhutan, Sri Lanka, and Viet Nam, which have achieved almost 100% electrification.

Despite these gains, more needs to be done. About 351 million in the Asia and Pacific region remain energy-poor as of 2017, and about 15% of those who reside in rural areas have no electricity access (IEA 2018). Table 1 shows a list of Asian Development Bank (ADB) developing member countries (DMCs) that have yet to achieve full national electrification; rural electrification is expectedly lower than urban.

ADB Responds to Energy Poverty in Asia and the Pacific

In 2009, ADB updated its energy policy to reflect the transformative role energy plays in overcoming economic poverty. ADB's *Energy Policy 2009* consists of three pillars, namely (i) promoting energy efficiency and renewable energy; (ii) maximizing access to energy for all; and (iii) promoting energy sector reform, capacity building, and governance. ADB has assumed a more direct role in providing reliable, adequate, and affordable energy to spur economic growth among its DMCs. Since 2013, ADB has pegged its annual clean energy investment to $2 billion.

Table 1. Electricity Access of Selected ADB Developing Member Countries

ADB Developing Member Country	Latest Data	Level of Electricity Access			Source
		% of Total Population	% of Rural Population	% of Urban Population	
Central and West Asia					
Afghanistan	2016	84	79	98	WB
Pakistan	2017	74	64	90	IEA
East Asia					
Mongolia	2017	91	73	99	IEA
Pacific					
Kiribati		85	82	88	
FSM		75	71	92	
Papua New Guinea	2016	23	15	73	WB
Solomon Islands		48	42	70	
Timor-Leste		63	49	92	
Vanuatu		58	46	91	
South Asia					
Bangladesh		80	73	93	
India	2017	87	82	98	IEA
Nepal		91	89	99	
Sri Lanka		100	100	100	
Southeast Asia					
Cambodia		61	50	97	
Indonesia		95	89	100	
Lao PDR	2017	94	91	100	IEA
Myanmar		56	46	79	
Philippines		88	80	98	

ADB = Asian Development Bank, FSM = Federated States of Micronesia, IEA = Inernational Energy Agency, Lao PDR = Lao People's Democratic Republic, WB = World Bank.
Sources: For Afghanistan and the Pacific countries: World Bank. *World Development Indicators*. https://databank.worldbank.org (accessed 24 June 2019). For Mongolia, Pakistan, and other countries in South Asia and Southeast Asia: International Energy Agency. 2018. *World Energy Outlook 2018*. Paris. https://doi.org/10.1787/weo-2018-en.

As part of the road map to enhance lending activities, ADB launched the Energy for All Initiative, also known as Energy for All. The initiative is a regional technical assistance program tasked to work with various regional departments within ADB to help increase their lending for energy access. From 2008 to 2017, this effort resulted in investments that totaled $8.4 billion and benefited 121 million people.

Recognizing the magnitude of the challenge, ADB reached out to other like-minded organizations to establish the Energy for All Partnership in 2009. The partnership agreed to and set an intermediary goal of providing modern energy access to 100 million people by 2015. This target was met and exceeded, as more than 125 million people were brought out of energy poverty at the end of 2015. In 2016, the partnership committed to a second goal, which is to provide modern energy access to additional 200 million people by 2020.

Energy for All also provides technical assistance to ADB DMC governments under its dual role as the Asia Pacific Hub for Sustainable Energy for All. It has supported these governments in formulating their strategies to achieve their Nationally Determined Contributions and international commitments under the Paris Agreement. Energy for All also supports the adoption of renewable energy sources in distributed electrification solutions for the Asia and Pacific region's energy-poor areas. It identifies companies and institutions that can implement commercially viable distributed electrification solutions, and enables them to access the financing they need to scale up their impact. The primary clients of Energy for All for its business acceleration and investment facilitation services are private companies that offer products and services that alleviate energy poverty in the Asia and Pacific region.

Mobilizing Distributed Electrification Solutions to the Frontiers of Energy Poverty

The expansion of the power grid has been the backbone of national electrification efforts in Asia for the past decade. Among these countries, a strong tradition of central governance has also contributed to successful national electrification because this enables significant amounts of public resources to be mobilized for large infrastructure projects in a short amount of time. The People's Republic of China and Viet Nam, which have achieved full electriciation, are prime examples.

In more complex geographies, the optimal electrification approach is not straightforward. Archipelagic countries like Indonesia (which spans about 14,000 islands) and the Philippines (which spans about 7,000 islands) are difficult to electrify through power grid expansion alone. Undersea cables are technically feasible, but only viable when connecting nearby islands with substantial electricity demand. Countries with extreme elevation, such as Nepal, face similar technical and economic constraints that render grid expansion infeasible. Many countries in the Asia and Pacific region have areas with similar extreme geographies that pose challenges to national electrification. To overcome these challenges and realize their national electrification targets, governments can deploy off-grid or distributed electrification modalities for remote and isolated areas where grid extension is not viable, and adopt renewable energy technologies that provide cost savings in the long run.

While rural electrification has always been a development priority, the evolution of energy storage, energy generation, smart meters, and internet connectivity creates new electrification solutions that compete with traditional grid connections. Interest on distributed electrification, such as off-grid and mini-grid solutions, is gaining ground with the realization that it could complement and supplement national electrification plans. Distributed electrification can be an option for remote areas where extending the grid is currently too costly. It may be a temporary or a permanent solution depending on the per capita energy consumption and socioeconomic status of the area. Distributed electrification could also accelerate the growth of electricity demand resulting in sooner grid extension or integration with nearby villages. REN21 (2017) summarizes the secondary benefits of distributed renewable energy systems (DRES):

(i)   Cost savings when compared to the grid in many markets

(ii)   Fuel availability and stability, and price predictability

(iii)   Modularity, flexibility, and rapid construction times

(iv)   Faster technological learning curves and rates of improvement compared to fossil fuels

(v)   Enhanced reliability and resilience

(vi)   Improved health through reductions in indoor air pollution

(vii)   Contribution to climate change mitigation

(viii) Reductions in deforestation and environmental degradation

(ix)   Positive effects on women's empowerment

(x)   Reduction of poverty among vulnerable groups

As developing Asia moves closer to universal electrification, the task involves the most challenging areas—remote, mountainous terrains, and isolated islands. To connect some 351 million people, the majority of whom are in rural areas, a combination of centralized and distributed electrification approaches, and adoption of renewable energy would have to be considered. While renewable energy policies and targets are in place for most DMCs, the legal, regulatory, and institutional environment for distributed renewable energy and mini-grids have to be developed. Distributed renewable energy electrification will not only help achieve universal access, it will also fulfill the commitments to mitigate climate change. This report presents a guide to the DMCs in deploying renewable energy systems (Figure 1).

Figure 1. Framework for Deploying Distributed Renewable Energy Systems

Regulatory, Institutional, and Market Scanning → Supply and Demand Analysis → Project Design Optimization → Project Implementation → Social, Economic, and Environmental Impact Assessment

Source: ADB.

With energy policymakers, development investors, and other stakeholders as intended audience, this report aims to

    (i) offer a manual for incorporating distributed electrification in national electrification programs,

    (ii) present techniques and tools that can be used to optimize utilization of renewable energy sources for off-grid electrification,

    (iii) present the case study of the Philippines' Cobrador Island hybrid solar photovoltaic (PV) mini-grid, and

    (iv) document the outcomes and lessons learned to contribute in mainstreaming solutions involving DRES.

The next four chapters provide an overview of the Energy for All experience in deploying technical solutions for renewable energy mini-grids and distributed power generation. The last two chapters focus on the Philippine case study of Cobrador Island's solar PV–diesel hybrid mini-grid. The report proceeds as follows:

Chapter 2 proposes a procedure to assess regulatory and institutional environment for the viability of renewable energy mini-grid and distributed electrification. A proposed market and regulatory assessment is presented in Box 1. While it is not a foolproof procedure, it provides an organized start for policymakers, development investors, and the private sector in determining the feasibility of undertaking such off-grid and distributed electrification projects in the various DMCs.

Chapter 3 analyzes the energy supply and demand scenario at subnational level using geospatial mapping techniques and the Multi-Tier Framework (MTF) for measuring energy access. For better understanding on how to conduct geospatial mapping, this chapter features Myanmar's map layers that help analyze existing power infrastructure, potential demand in off-grid areas population density, and available renewable energy resources that may be tapped. A detailed supply and demand analysis of households' electricity services could be performed using the MTF approach. Knowing the existing and aspired tier gives light to possible renewable energy technology options. The chapter lists renewable energy solutions—which had Energy for All involvement—that could be deployed in off-grid areas.

Chapter 4 focuses on finding the least-cost technology option for off-grid sites. Modeling tools, including Hybrid Optimization of Multiple Energy Resources (HOMER), are presented for rapid cost assessment and selection of the least-cost option.

Chapter 5 recounts an early iteration of the methodology to the Philippines. The Energy for All Initiative helped the National Electrification Administration of the Philippines (NEA) explore the applicability of renewable energy mini-grids in off-grid areas within the distribution franchise areas of electric cooperatives. A solar PV–diesel hybrid mini-grid was implemented in the island of Cobrador to demonstrate that DRES can provide Tier 5 level of energy access.

Chapter 6 assesses the social, economic, and environmental impacts of installing solar PV in Cobrador Island. Findings are based on interviews and surveys conducted a year after the hybrid mini-grid was commisioned, and simulations of impact factors.

Chapter 7 concludes with some general key points, lessons, and best practices from the Cobrador Island case study.

2 Regulatory and Institutional Environment

The regulatory and institutional environment influences the feasibility and growth potential of renewable energy mini-grids and distributed electrification. Many countries in the Asia and Pacific region have energy policies, strategies, and programs, yet 351 million remain unelectrified—many of whom are in remote and isolated areas that are beyond the reach of grid electrification. DRES are alternative solutions but would require special attention and support from the government as they are generally more difficult to implement than traditional grid-extension projects (Terrado, Cabraal, and Mukherjee 2008).

Most rural electrification programs are government-led and implemented as social welfare programs using public funds or support from multilateral donor organizations. While significant progress have been made by government-led initiatives, private sector participation can help bridge the investment gap to achieve universal energy access. Private sector participation primarily depends on commercial viability, which is often not the case in island and remote areas of ADB DMCs. The government's policies, regulations, and support could alter the game through subsidies and incentives and technical assistance.

A sound and comprehensive long-term electrification and management plan includes off-grid renewable energy systems as a medium for off-grid electrication, and highlights that the off-grid market is a different and separate entity from the on-grid market. For off-grid private sector participants, light-handed regulatory measures are recommended to simplify operations and limit the cost of doing business while adequately protecting consumers (Terrado, Cabraal, and Mukherjee 2008).

A robust institutional framework dedicated for electrification can support private sector players and provide a clear direction for the achievement of targets. Often it is a national agency that lead electrification efforts. The role of local governments is undeniable for energy access in remote areas. Compared to national agencies, local government units have more immediate access and have a better understanding of the energy needs and resources of the site. Building local capacity for energy planning or even awareness raising on DRES can facilitate provision of access in off-grid sites.

Institutional and governance structures should emphasize training and capacity development for all stakeholders; stress direct involvement and clearly defined roles of local governments, communities, and other stakeholders; provide options and processes for financial incentives and subsidies, financing, and investments (public and private sector), and determine tariffs and revenue streams. It is equally essential to build local capacity to develop, implement, and operate DRES to enhance replicability and ensure the sustainable operation of systems. Private clean energy companies are ideal channels for building local capacity in operating and maintaining systems. They have the expertise in building community-level skills to ensure regular maintenance and minor repairs on project sites.

Several indicators may be used to evaluate the regulatory and institutional frameworks for energy access of a country. Understanding where the gaps are will help government formulate more enabling policies to attract and support private sector players in off-grid electrification. Some of the indicators that may be used are listed below, which is a subset of the full list of Regulatory Indicators for Sustainable Energy that was developed to compare national policy and regulatory frameworks for sustainable energy (World Bank 2017).

(i) Existence of a national electrification program
- Is a time-bound target set for off-grid electrification or energy access?
- Are there programs that support the development of distributed systems?

(ii) Legal framework for distributed electrification
- Are distributed systems legally allowed to operate in the country?
- Can distributed systems be owned and operated by private operators?
- Do the regulations differ by size or capacity of systems?

(iii) Ability to charge cost-reflective tariffs
- Can distributed system operators charge a different tariff from the national tariff?

(iv) Financial incentives
- Are there subsidies or other funding mechanisms to secure viability gap funding?
- Are there specific financing facilities available to support energy providers?

(v) Standards and quality
- Are there electric safety standards?

A proposed framework is presented in Box 1 that could help assess the regulatory environment and market demand in the DMCs for off-grid and distributed electrification.

Box 1. Methodology for Market and Regulatory Environment Scanning

This assessment is organized into three categories. First is the size of the market demand for electrification in rural areas. The bigger the rural population, the higher the weight. Rural areas were given more weight than urban areas since rural areas are more optimally served by distributed electrification options compared to urban areas. The assessment only considers rural population since urban communities usually have higher population densities and are nearer power grids. The second category is the existence of an enabling environment for national electrification. This is exemplified by a national electrification plan with clear, time-bound targets. A premium is given to countries that specify interim electrification goals and have dedicated programs for rural electrification. Finally, the third category pertains to how competitive the market is for new entrants that provide alternative electrification solutions. Countries with a comprehensive policy in favor of renewables receive a higher rating because such policy enhances the competitiveness of distributed renewable electrification solutions, which are based on these technologies. Fossil fuel subsidies reflect negatively on a country's rating because it lowers the price of electricity to levels where renewable energy-based solutions may not be competitive.

1. **Market demand** ranks countries based on the size of their unelectrified rural population.

(a) The equation to compute the market demand for **rural electrification** is:

Total National Population	X	Percentage in Rural Areas	X	Percentage of Unelectrified Rural Population	=	**Market Demand for Rural Electrification**

(b) The equation to compute the score for **market demand** is:

$$\left[\frac{\text{Market Demand for Rural Electrification (Country A)}}{\text{Market Demand for Electrification in Rural Areas (India)*}} \right] \times \text{Category Weight (30\%)} \times 100 = \text{Market Demand Score}$$

*Note: Since rural India has the most number of unelectrified rural population at approximately 196 million in 2016 (*World Bank World Development Indicators*), it is used as the baseline from which the scores of the other countries are derived.

2. **Enabling environment** ranks a country based on the clarity of their long-term and short-term national electrification targets, and the existence of a program for rural electrification.

    (a) Countries that have long-term electrification targets receive the full weight of 30%.
    (b) Countries that have short-term electrification targets receive the full weight of 30%.
    (c) A higher weight of 40% is given to countries with rural electrification programs since these directly enhance the success of energy access projects.
    (d) The equation to compute the score for enabling environment is:

$$\left[\begin{array}{c} \text{Long-term} \\ \text{Electrification} \\ \text{Targets (30\%)} \end{array} + \begin{array}{c} \text{Short-term} \\ \text{Electrification} \\ \text{Targets (30\%)} \end{array} + \begin{array}{c} \text{Rural} \\ \text{Electrification} \\ \text{Programs} \\ \text{(40\%)} \end{array} \right] \times \begin{array}{c} \text{Category} \\ \text{Weight} \\ \text{(30\%)} \end{array} \times 100 = \begin{array}{c} \textbf{Enabling} \\ \textbf{Environment} \\ \textbf{Score} \end{array}$$

3. **Market competitiveness** ranks a country based on the comprehensiveness of their renewable energy policy, the extent that private companies can participate in power generation and distribution, and the existence of subsidies for fossil fuels.

    (a) A comprehensive renewable energy policy would have provisions for the following: (i) feed-in-tariff, (ii) competitive bidding, (iii) guaranteed offtake, (iv) priority dispatch (v) self-consumption scheme, (vi) income tax holiday, (vii) importation tax deduction, (viii) VAT deduction, (ix) renewable energy certificates, and (x) concessional financing. A country receives 1 point for each of the 10 provisions contained in their renewable energy policy. The total score is then multiplied by 25%, the weight of this subcategory.
    (b) Distributed renewable energy electrification companies can only offer their products and services to the end-user if the government allows private companies to participate in energy generation and distribution. Having the legal provisions for both generation and distribution are required to receive a full score of 50% for this subcategory. Without either, a country receives a score of zero.
    (c) Countries that have fossil fuel subsidy receives a score of zero, while those that do not receive the full score of 25% for this subcategory.

The equation to compute the score for market competitiveness is:

$$\left[\begin{array}{c} \text{Comprehensiveness} \\ \text{of Renewable Energy} \\ \text{Policy} \\ \text{(25\%)} \end{array} + \begin{array}{c} \text{Private Sector} \\ \text{Participation in} \\ \text{the Power Sector} \\ \text{(50\%)} \end{array} + \begin{array}{c} \text{Fossil Fuel} \\ \text{Subsidy} \\ \text{(25\%)} \end{array} \right] \times \begin{array}{c} \text{Category} \\ \text{Weight} \\ \text{(40\%)} \end{array} \times 100 = \begin{array}{c} \textbf{Market} \\ \textbf{Competitiveness} \\ \textbf{Score} \end{array}$$

Source: ADB.

3 Supply and Demand Analysis

Where pure grid expansion is not a viable path because of economic or geographic reasons, adding a distributed electrification component to the national electrification plan could alleviate a country's journey to universal electricity access. Tools are available to understand the energy supply and demand of a country for informed policy and investment decisions. Geospatial mapping can clarify the size of the distributed electrification market, while the MTF for Measuring Energy Access can provide a detailed analysis of the energy usage and supply down to the electricity service levels, and assist in setting country- and area-specific electrification targets. Knowing the existing and aspired electricity service levels, the type of technology could be chosen from an array of options in the market. The Energy for All Initiative has been involved in a number of distributed renewable energy solutions in Asia, which are outlined and described in this chapter.

Geospatial Mapping

A geospatial map is a useful visualization tool for electrification planning that reconciles data sets on energy supply and demand with the location wherein they apply. Digitally, each indicator of energy demand and supply, such as number of households and solar irradiation data, are connected to Global Positioning System (GPS) coordinates. Once aggregated, these data sets can be visualized into separate map layers that can be overlaid with each other to aid in comparative analysis and decision-making.

Geospatial mapping can identify unelectrified villages and provide information on available local resources and nearby infrastructure to estimate the potential for off-grid investments. Through its various layers that are superimposed on the primary map, geospatial mapping approximates energy demand and customers' capacity to pay, as well as the energy supply through the available resources. Possible markets or users of DRES are populations living outside the service area of existing generation, transmission, and distribution infrastructure. The parameters—population, existing infrastructure, and natural resources—are made to interact to analyze possible off-grid solutions. Box 2 demonstrates the map layers that an ADB project developed across Myanmar's three states.[1]

---

[1] ADB. 2014. *Technical Assistance to the Republic of the Union of Myanmar for the Off-Grid Renewable Energy Demonstration Project.* Manila. (Technical Assistance 8657). https://www.adb.org/projects/47128-001/main.

Box 2. Supply and Demand Analysis through Geospatial Mapping – Myanmar

The geospatial mapping of the three states of Myanmar—Magway, Mandalay, and Sagaing—was undertaken under Asian Development Bank (ADB) Technical Assistance 8657: Myanmar Off-Grid Renewable Energy Demonstration Project. The analysis explored the status of electrification, energy infrastructure, renewable resources, and off-grid opportunities in the three states. The following map layers show the data visualization capability of geospatial mapping.

1. **Creating the base maps**
   1.1. The **political map layer** is the primary map illustrating the country's internal and external territorial boundaries, and the locations of geographic features like rivers, lakes, and mountains.
   1.2. The **elevation layer** contains information about the altitude of each location, which can be overlaid with the drainage network layer and the precipitation layer to estimate the hydropower potential of a site and cost of expanding the transmission and distribution network.
   1.3. The **satellite layer** contains high-altitude and high-resolution images from which information on geographical features and energy demand could be derived.

2. **Estimating the demand**
   2.1. The **villages layer** contains the Global Positioning System (GPS) coordinates and population size of the villages, and among its features is identifying villages' distance from the transmission and distribution network plotted in the powerlines layer.
   2.2. The **clusters layer** is a group of one or more villages in the village layer that are no more than 1 kilometer away from each other, and useful for identifying areas for distributed energy solutions that can distribute electricity efficiently beyond 1 kilometer.

3. **Determining the off-grid opportunities**
   3.1. The **powerlines layer** contains the GPS coordinates of all the nodes that form the existing transmission and distribution grid, which can be used to exclude villages and village clusters that will be connected to the grid in the near future and show the least cost of electrification of expanding the grid to each unelectrified region.
   3.2. The **diesel generators layer** contains the GPS coordinates of diesel-based mini-grids suggesting potential sites for renewable energy hybridization, and capacity to pay and creditworthiness of the village or village cluster a mini-grid serves.
   3.3. The **ADB mini-grids layer** shows the locations of the 12 solar photovoltaic (PV) mini-grids in Magway, Mandalay, and Sagaing suggesting the villages and village clusters' capacity to pay.
   3.4. The **microfinance institution (MFI) network layer** indicates the creditworthiness of an unelectrified village or village cluster, that is, if multiple MFIs have been operating for an extended period.

4. **Estimating the renewable energy resources**
   4.1. The **drainage network layer** identifies junction points with high water flow rates since these are good predictors of hydropower potential.
   4.2. The **precipitation layer** visualizes the average amount of rainfall annually, that is, a high degree of rainfall may benefit from hydropower generation if the drainage network in the area diverts water to a nearby river system.
   4.3. The **potential hydropower sites layer** is a multidimensional analysis that contains the coordinates of potential hydropower sites that have a favorable combination of elevation (from the elevation layer), precipitation (from the precipitation layer) and water flow (from the drainage network layer).
   4.4. The **solar irradiance layer** visualizes the amount of solar irradiation in a target area, which could be possible sites for a solar PV mini-grid, or a solar PV–diesel hybrid mini-grid.
   4.5. The **biomass groundnut layer** locates townships where groundnut—a feedstock for biomass boilers to produce baseload electricity—is produced as an agro-industrial by-product.
   4.6. The **biomass rice layer** locates townships that produce rice husk—can be used to produce electricity through biomass gasification—as an agro-industrial by-product.

Source: ADB.

Multi-Tier Framework for Measuring Energy Access

Developed by a consortium of international development agencies and programs,[2] the MTF has redefined the traditional binary measurement of having or not having energy access, to a spectrum of service levels from Tier 0 (no service) to Tier 5 (full service). The MTF not only measures whether users receive energy services, but also whether services are adequate, available when needed, reliable, of good quality, affordable, legal, and safe.

Information from the MTF can be used to analyze current energy usage and provide other relevant supply and demand data; prioritize investments, and interventions and make informed policy decisions; set country- and area-specific targets for universal access; track progress in providing access to reliable, affordable, and modern energy services; and capture the various modes of access delivery from grid to off-grid and fuels used.[3] Off-grid sites may be classified according to the required or aspired level of electrification, and possible distributed renewable or hybrid technologies could be identified based on the classification.

The following tables present the multi-tier matrix for measuring access to household electricity supply and electricity services, and the multi-tier matrix for measuring electricity consumption (Bhatia and Angelou 2015). These could be cross-referenced with the table on technology options (found on the next section) in choosing what is suitable for a remote area or community. Tier 1 to Tier 2 levels of consumption characterize households that primarily use electricity on small appliances that provide comfort or entertainment. At least a Tier 3 level of electrification is required for medium-sized appliances that can be used for product end uses.

Distributed Renewable Energy Technologies

Renewable energy generation capacity in the global energy mix had grown for almost 2 decades. In 2000, solar photovoltaic (PV) and wind only accounted for a combined 32 terawatt-hour (TWh), and 17 years later, the generation capacity of solar PV was 435 TWh and wind was 1,545 TWh. The International Energy Agency (2018) estimated that the installed power generation capacity from solar PV and wind, together with hydropower, already accounts for 32% globally and is projected to increase to 51% by 2040.[4]

---

[2] The MTF is developed by World Bank–Energy Sector Management Assistance Program, in consultation with development agencies and programs including Energising Development, Lighting Africa, Practical Action, the Global Alliance for Clean Cookstoves, the United Nations Development Programme, the United Nations Industrial Development Organization, World Bank, and the World Health Organization.

[3] M. Bhatia and N. Angelou. 2016. *Energy Access Diagnostic Report Based on the Multi-Tier Framework: Beyond Connections. Energy Sector Management Assistance Program.* https://www.esmap.org/node/56715; and Sustainable Energy for All. *Beyond Connections: Energy Access Redefined – Introducing Multi-Tier Approach to Measuring Energy Access.* https://www.seforall.org/sites/default/files/Beyond-Connections-Introducing-Multi-Tier-Framework-for-Tracking-Energy-Access.pdf.

[4] International Energy Agency. Based on the New Policies Scenario in the World Energy Outlook 2018. Figures and percentages were obtained from https://www.iea.org/weo.

Table 2. Multi-Tier Matrix for Measuring Access to Household Electricity Supply

Attributes		Tier 0	Tier 1	Tier 2	Tier 3	Tier 4	Tier 5
Peak Capacity	Power capacity ratings (in W or daily Wh)		Min 3 W	Min 50 W	Min 200 W	Min 800 W	Min 2 kW
			Min 12 Wh	Min 200 Wh	Min 1.0 kWh	Min 3.4 kWh	Min 8.2 kWh
	OR Services		Lighting of 1,000 lmhr/day	Electrical lighting, air circulation, television, and phone charging are possible			
Availability (Duration)	Hours per day		Min 4 hrs	Min 4 hrs	Min 8 hrs	Min 16 hrs	Min 23 hrs
	Hours per evening		Min 1 hr	Min 2 hrs	Min 3 hrs	Min 4 hrs	Min 4 hrs
Reliability						Max 14 disruptions per week	Max 3 disruptions per week of total duration <2 hrs
Quality						Voltage problems do not affect the use of desired appliances	
Affordability						Cost of a standard consumption package of 365 kWh/year <5% of household income	
Legality						Bill is paid to the utility, prepaid card seller, or authorized representative	
Health and Safety						Absence of past accidents and perception of high risk in the future	

hr = hour, kWh = kilowatt-hour, lmhr = lumen-hour, W = watt, Wh = watt-hour.

Source: M. Bhatia and N. Angelou. 2015. *Beyond Connections - Energy Access Redefined: Technical Report*. Energy Sector Management Assistance Program. Washington, DC: World Bank Group. http://documents.worldbank.org/curated/en/650971468180259602/Beyond-connections-energy-access-redefined-technical-report.

Table 3. Multi-Tier Matrix for Measuring Access to Household Electricity Services

Item	Tier 0	Tier 1	Tier 2	Tier 3	Tier 4	Tier 5
Tier Criteria		Task lighting and phone charging	General lighting, phone charging, television, and fan (if needed)	Tier 2 and any medium-power appliances	Tier 3 and any high-power appliances	Tier 2 and any very high-power appliances

Source: M. Bhatia and N. Angelou. 2015. *Beyond Connections - Energy Access Redefined: Technical Report.* Energy Sector Management Assistance Program. Washington, DC: World Bank Group. http://documents.worldbank.org/curated/en/650971468180259602/Beyond-connections-energy-access-redefined-technical-report.

Table 4. Multi-Tier Matrix for Measuring Household Electricity Consumption

Item	Tier 0	Tier 1	Tier 2	Tier 3	Tier 4	Tier 5
Annual consumption levels, in kWhs		≥4.5	≥73	≥365	≥1,250	≥3,000
Daily consumption levels, in Whs		≥12.0	≥200	≥1,000	≥3,425	≥8,219

kWh = kilowatt-hour, Wh = watt-hour.

Source: M. Bhatia and N. Angelou. 2015. *Beyond Connections - Energy Access Redefined: Technical Report.* Energy Sector Management Assistance Program. Washington, DC: World Bank Group. http://documents.worldbank.org/curated/en/650971468180259602/Beyond-connections-energy-access-redefined-technical-report.

Development of renewable energy technologies will continue with emphasis on the provision of sustainable modern energy for all. Locally available and virtually free, the operating costs of renewable energy have a significant advantage over fossil fuel-based solutions, such as diesel generators and kerosene lamps. Leading companies in the energy access sector are building on this inherent advantage and innovating further to deliver cheaper renewable energy to end users.

An indicator—although not directly comparable to small off-grid installations—utility-scale solar PV has had the most rapid decline in the levelized cost of electricity (LCOE). The total global weighted average cost of utility scale solar PV projects fell by 65% from 2012 to 2017. Recent auctions for solar PV offered some of the lowest recorded prices, such as $24 per megawatt-hour (MWh) in the United Arab Emirates, $27 per MWh in India, $20 per MWh in Mexico, and $18 per MWh in Saudi Arabia (IEA 2018).

The cost of energy storage will also decline as production capacity increases and more common raw material elements are used. Among the commercially deployed energy storage technologies, lithium-ion batteries still provide the lowest levelized cost of storage (LCOS) across the various use cases in peak load replacement, electricity distribution, and microgrids. Increased mass manufacturing capacity in the People's Republic of China, Thailand, and the United States within the next 5 years will bolster the cost leadership of lithium-ion batteries.

Literature on renewable energy mini-grids and distributed generation is rich on the available technology options. Different types of DRES where Energy for All had been involved are presented in Table 5. They vary in complexity and extent of energy access that can be delivered.

1. **Micro-hydropower.** *Dhostekhor Khola Micro-Hydropower Pilot Project (Nepal).* ADB has supported the implementation of a 50-kW community-based small hydro pilot project in Sikha Village Development Committee of Myagdi district in the Western Development Region of Nepal. The pilot project powers five community-owned lodges, all located at an elevation above 3,000 meters (m) right below Annapurna South Peak, along the Annapurna Dhaulagi Community Trekking Route. The revenues from selling the electricity to the lodges will be used to cover the cost of operating the hydro plant with the excess revenues to financially support five local schools in the area. The hydropower plant is owned by the community and was financed through ADB, community contributions, a local bank, District Development Committee Myagdi and the Annapurna Conservation Area Project, Nepal Tourism Board, and Huguenin Rallapalli Foundation of the United States.

   Rural Community-Based Micro-Hydropower Development in Mindanao (Philippines). The technical assistance project consisted of the establishment and capacity building of community-based organizations, the development of livelihood enterprises and activities, the establishment and initial management of financial tools (revolving fund) and the procurement and installation of two micro-hydropower plants in Barangay Dalupan (25 kW) and in Barangay Getsemane (30 kW). The plants are operated under a net metering arrangement, a first in the Philippines. Under this arrangement, the communities use the generated power for business activities and sell excess power to distribution utilities. The generated revenue is used to cover the operation and maintenance costs, and support livelihood activities within the community. The community-based organizations and their members were trained to operate and maintain the power plants, and manage the revolving funds.

2. **Solar PV Mini-Grid.** *Khotang Micro-grid Project (Nepal).* The rural micro-grid pilot provides reliable energy access for households and entrepreneurial activities in three rural communities in Okhaldunga and Khotang districts through a collaborative project between the local community, ADB, DOEN Foundation, Nepal government's Alternative Energy Promotion Center, and Gham Power, a private company. The project deployed a 35-kilowatt (kW) solar micro-grid system that powers 31 rural businesses and 61 households. A special purpose vehicle (SPV) was formed, which is co-owned by Gham Power and the local community. Recently, another 37 kW of solar PV was added in two of the villages to provide power to two new telecom towers installed by Ncell, Nepal's largest private telecom company. The additional capacity also provides power to households and businesses that were not served by the initial system.

Table 5. Technology Options and Energy Service Providers in the Energy for All Partnership

Technology Options	Description	E4All Project Power System	Proponent/ Energy Service Providers	Level of Electrification[a]
Lighting Utility	DC electricity is generated by solar PV panels, and distributed to households for basic lighting and mobile phone charging. To avoid significant distribution losses, the size of the community must not exceed a 1-kilometer radius.		Mera Gao Power (India)	Up to Tier 2
		Dhostekhor Khola Micro–Hydropower Pilot Project (Nepal) *Isolated mini-grid*	Local community	Up to Tier 5
Run–of–River Mini–hydropower	Community level mini-hydropower plants in the E4ALL pipeline range from 180 kW to 1.5 MW. These are connected to transmission and distribution networks that can provide up to a Tier 5 level of electrification.	Rural Community–Based Micro–Hydropower Development in Mindanao (Philippines)	Rural cooperative in the township of Dalupan and Getsemane	Initially up to Tier 4. Upgraded to Tier 5 after interconnection to the primary grid.
Solar Home System	A solar home system is a modular energy generation system that is designed to power a single location. It comes with a solar PV panel, battery and wiring to connect LED lights, LCD screens or other low-wattage electronics. Solar home systems normally range from 5 W to 200 W. The larger systems can provide Tier 3 level of electricity.		E4All Partner: Mega Renewables Corporation (Philippines) Simpa Energy (India), Boond (India), One Renewable Energy Enterprises (Philippines), SOLARIC (Bangladesh), Gham Power (Nepal), E-Hands Energy Pvt. Ltd. (India)	Up to Tier 5
Solar PV	Solar PV systems may be rooftop or ground mounted. The DC electricity is converted to AC with an inverter and may be directly fed to the end user or to a distribution grid.	Khotang Micro-grid Project (Nepal) *Isolated mini-grid*	Gham Power and Local Community	Up to Tier 4

Technology Options	Description	E4All Project Power System	Proponent/Energy Service Providers	Level of Electrification[a]
		Cobrador Island Solar Hybrid Project (Philippines) *Isolated mini-grid*	Romblon Electric Cooperative	Up to Tier 5
Solar PV–Diesel Hybrid Mini-grid	Solar PV panels are integrated with diesel generator sets to generate electricity for 24 hours a day, 7 days a week. Both generation assets are connected to an isolated distribution grid, through which electricity is transmitted to households and microenterprises.	Malalison Island Solar Hybrid Project (Philippines) *Isolated mini-grid*	Aklan Electric Cooperative	Up to Tier 5
		Off-Grid Renewable Energy Demonstration Project (Myanmar) *Isolated mini-grid*	Local Community	Up to Tier 4
			Sun-eee (Cambodia), Gham Power (Nepal), E-Hands Energy Pvt. Ltd. (India)	Up to Tier 5
Swarm Electrification	Swarm Electrification creates a micro-grid among households that utilizes surplus electricity from Solar Home Systems to power other households. A smart meter is used to monitor the "trading" of electricity among households.	Swarm Electrification Project (Bangladesh) *Swarm electrification system*	SOLShare (Bangladesh)	Up to Tier 3
Wind–Solar Hybrid System	This hybrid system combines the generations from wind mill and solar energy panel, and usually has low capacities ranging from 1 to 10 kW.	Wind–Solar Hybrid Power System (Nepal) *Isolated mini-grid*	Nepal government's Alternative Energy Promotion Center	Up to Tier 3

AC = alternating current, DC = direct current, E4All = Energy for All, kW = kilowatt, LCD = liquid crystal display, LED = light-emitting diode, Ltd = Limited, MW = megawatt, PV = photovoltaic, Pvt = Private, W = watt.

Note: [a] Energy access is measured in a tiered-spectrum, that is improving attributes of energy supply—quality, reliability, affordability, safety, and availability—leads to higher tiers of access. Tier 0 is no access, while Tier 5 is the highest level of access.

Source: Energy for All Initiative, ADB.

3. **Solar PV–Diesel Hybrid Mini-Grid.** *Cobrador Island Hybrid Solar PV Project (Philippines).* ADB and the Korea Energy Agency (KEA) supported the development of a mini-grid system to hybridize existing diesel-based electricity generation with renewable energy in Cobrador Island, Romblon. The mini-grid system combines a 30-kW solar PV installation, 190-kWh lithium-ion batteries for storage, and 15-kW diesel generator with a power control system. The pilot project extended electricity supply in the island from 8 to 24 hours, and provides service to all 260 homes, the community's health center, elementary school, and village hall, and supports local industries like fishing, small retail stores, and artisanal marble processing. Romblon Electric Cooperative (ROMELCO), a nonprofit distribution utility mandated to distribute electricity in Cobrador Island, implements the project.

    Malalison Island Solar Hybrid Project (Philippines). The pilot project is a joint initiative of ADB and Antique Electric Cooperative, a nonprofit electric cooperative given the franchise to distribute electricity in the entire province of Antique. The project aims to hybridize a diesel-based system with renewable energy, and extend electricity service from 4 to 24 hours per day for 200 consumers and small establishments in Malalison Island. It will also replace the Antique Electric Cooperative's existing 25-kW diesel power generation facility with 50-kW diesel generator, and hybridize it with 50-kW solar PV backed-up with a 273-kWh lithium-ion battery system. The project pilot tests and demonstrates two innovative approaches in generating and distributing electricity in off-grid islands: the (i) joint venture model between an electric cooperative (EC) and a private sector company as investment partner, and (ii) use of a pre-paid metering system in a remote island setting to improve collection.

4. **Solar PV and Solar PV–Diesel Hybrid Mini-Grids.** *Off-Grid Renewable Energy Demonstration Project (Myanmar).* Under the project, solar mini-grids systems were installed in 12 villages located in the country's Dry Zone (Magway, Mandalay, and Sagaing regions). The mini-grids consist of 10 stand-alone projects, 1 diesel hybrid system and 1 project built to grid standards that can be connected to the national grid when it arrives in the village. Solar PV capacities range from 4.9 kW to 13 kW, while batteries are in the range of 18 kWh to 115 kWh. The ADB project funded 80% of the installation costs, while the villagers contributed the remaining 20%. For each community, a village electrification committee was established to collect payment from the villagers.

5. **Solar PV Swarm Electrification.** *Swarm Electrification Project (Bangladesh).* ADB has collaborated with ME SOLShare, a company that developed an innovative technology and a concept called "Swarm Electrification" where excess solar energy from solar home systems (SHS) in a community is diverted to poorer households that cannot afford an SHS of their own. A marketplace enables community members to acquire excess energy from SHS owners who sell their excess energy. The supported pilot project has connected about 200 consumers. Swarm electrification proposes a distributed bottom–up sharing infra-system by linking together individual stand-alone energy systems to form a mini-grid that can eventually interconnect with present infrastructure.

6. **Wind–Solar Hybrid System.** *Wind–Solar Hybrid Power System (Nepal).* ADB supported the installation of a wind–solar hybrid power system in Hariharpurgadi village of Sindhuli district to provide electricity services to 83 households through 20-kW wind turbines and 15-kW peak solar PV. The system produces 110 kWh of energy per day, which can meet the electricity demand of the community. This project is implemented by Alternative Energy Promotion Center and financed through ADB's South Asia Subregional Economic Cooperation Power System Expansion Project. The project was partly financed by the Government of Nepal, the Scaling up of Renewable Energy Program under the Climate Investment Fund, and the local community.

The selection of the technology option to deploy will depend primarily on energy demand and availability of resources. Geospatial maps can analyze the energy scenarios of a country's unelectrified regions and identify a village or cluster of villages that distributed renewable electrification can serve. In-depth supply and demand analysis can be accomplished with a multi-tier approach to measuring energy access. Understanding of off-grid sites is important for site-specific strategic electrification planning. Energy demand maps and multi-tier energy access assessments provide governments and private sector useful information for off-grid electrification planning.

4

Finding the Least-Cost Technology Option

Transitioning from Site Selection to Site Optimization

Various factors influence the selection of the technology to serve off-grid sites. Among them are available resources, energy demand, costs, and end-user characteristics. Since energy demand is thinner and demand growth is slower in off-grid areas, finding the most cost-effective system to supply electricity is critical in enhancing the financial viability of operating the system.

LCOE is the commonly used measure of the competitiveness of different technology or system options. It is the average life cycle cost, including all capital, replacement, and operation and maintenance (O&M) costs, per kWh of useful energy.[5] Cost assessment becomes more rigorous as the system becomes more complex such as in renewable energy hybrid mini-grids. The power output from renewable energy is intermittent and non-dispatchable, making it more challenging to simulate least-cost performance and to calculate the associated life cycle costs.

Several modeling tools have been developed to analyze the costs of electrification options (Table 6). These tools vary in scope and capabilities that may be broadly categorized as simulation, optimization, and investment optimization. A tool may be selected depending on the level of planning or analysis to be done or may be used to complement another. These modeling tools can be used for national level planning, site-specific system design, upgrading system capacity, or shifting to renewable energy generation.

The tools can be used to plan for new installations in sites with no previous access, or for upgrading the capacities of existing facilities. Sites with lower electrification tier will eventually upgrade to Tier 5 access as a product of economic development. Table 7 describes how a Tier 5 level of energy can be achieved by communities that have been previously powered by solutions that offer lower-tier levels of electrification. For some, such as lighting utility and swarm electrification, the path to achieving Tier 5 electrification is constrained by technology limitations. Therefore communities that begin with these solutions may consider shifting to a different technology to attain Tier 5 electrification. Pathways toward Tier 5 electrification can be simulated to determine the most cost-effective system design.

---

[5]   The LCOE is often used to compare generating facilities but can be expanded to include all stages of electricity delivery.

Table 6. Modeling Tools for Energy System Planning and Analysis

Model	Description	Geographic Area	Simulation	Optimization Operation	Optimization Investment
AIM/End-use	Cost minimization modeling tool for energy planning	National, regional		✓	✓
ASIM	Simulates solar/diesel power system operations and conducts analysis of its technical and financial performance, ideal for system design	Community	✓		
FINPLAN (Financial Analysis of Electric Sector Expansion Plans)	Assesses the financial viability of projects, taking into account financial sources				✓
GEOSIM	Determines the most cost-effective electricity generation options	Community			✓
HOMER (Hybrid Optimization of Multiple Energy Resources)	Performs simulations and optimization to find the least-cost system configuration	Local community	✓	✓	✓
LEAP (Long Range Energy Alternatives Planning)	Modeling tool used to track energy consumption, production and resource extraction	National, regional	✓		✓
MARKAL/TIMES	Economic- environmental optimization model for least-cost planning of energy systems	National, regional			✓
GIZ (Deutsche Gesellschaft für Internationale Zusammenarbeit) Mini-grid Builder	Performs energy demand calculations and required generation capacity	Community	✓		
MESSAGE (Model for Energy Supply Strategy Alternatives and their General Environmental Impact)	Medium- to long-term energy system planning, energy policy analysis and scenario development	Global		✓	✓
Network Planner	Used for least-cost planning for grid, mini-grid, and off-grid systems	Community, national			✓
Paladin DesignBase	Simulation platform for modeling, analyzing, and optimizing power system performance	National	✓	✓	

Continued on page 22.

Continued from page 21.

Model	Description	Geographic Area	Simulation	Optimization	
				Operation	Investment
RETScreen	Used to determine whether or not a proposed renewable energy, or energy efficiency project is financially viable	User-defined	✓		
REDEO (Rural Electrification Decentralized Energy Options)	Handles off-grid systems used to compare various distributed power generation options	Local, community	✓		
WASP (Wien Automatic System Planning)	Expansion plan optimization model for electricity generation	National, regional	✓	✓	✓

Sources: R. M. Shrestha and J. S. Acharya. 2015. *Sustainable Energy Access Planning: A Framework.* Manila: ADB. https://www.adb.org/sites/default/files/publication/160740/sustainable-energy-access-planning-fw.pdf; International Atomic Energy Agency. Energy Modelling Tools. https://www.iaea.org/topics/energy-planning/energy-modelling-tools (accessed January 2019); Deutsche Gesellschaft für Internationale Zusammenarbeit (GIZ). 2016. *What Size Shall It Be? A Guide to Mini-grid Sizing and Demand Forecasting.* Nairobi, Kenya. https://www.giz.de/en/downloads/Sizing_handbook_150dpi_for_web.pdf.

Table 7. Power Systems Deployed by Selected Technology Options

Technology Options	Level of Electrification	Power System Type	Upgrading Delivery to Tier 5 Energy Access
Solar PV–Diesel Hybrid Mini-grid	Up to Tier 5	Hybrid Mini-Grid	The power generation capacity of the system must be enough to supply the demand.
Lighting Utility	Up to Tier 2	Mini-Grid	The system must be upgraded to a solar PV–diesel hybrid or a solar PV-ESS facility.
Solar Home System	Up to Tier 3	Stand-alone System	The capacity of the solar PV modules and the battery must be increased to supply household demand, which may not be economical for entire villages. Upgrading to a solar PV–diesel hybrid mini-grid may be cost-effective.
Swarm Electrification	Up to Tier 4	Mini-Grid	Increase number of participating solar home systems in the swarm to increase capacity. Convert to a solar PV–diesel hybrid or a solar PV-ESS mini-grid.
Run-of-River Hydropower	Up to Tier 5	Mini-Grid	The power generation capacity of the hydropower turbines must be enough to supply demand.

ESS = energy storage system, PV = photovoltaic.
Source: ADB.

HOMER for Project Design Optimization

HOMER is a modeling software developed by the National Renewable Energy Laboratory (NREL) that analyzes performance and costs of power systems. HOMER performs three principal tasks: simulation, optimization, and sensitivity analysis. Its simulations follow a cost-minization principle to find technically feasible system that will meet the demand. For example, when simulating a solar PV–diesel hybrid system with a battery bank, it will prioritize dispatch of stored energy during nighttime rather than running the generator set, which will entail fuel costs. The optimization process then ranks all technically viable systems according to the lowest cost by default. HOMER can perform sensitivity analysis by investigating the effects of external parameters, such as diesel price or demand growth (Lambert, Gilman, and Lilienthal 2006). Such modeling capability enables developers to make sound design decisions in a short amount of time. It has gained preference among practitioners due in part to the wide range of components it can simulate (renewable energy, dispatchable energy, storage, and converters).

HOMER takes a bottom–up modeling approach where the simulations depend on site-specific conditions, including the load profile and renewable energy resources, to generate technical and economic information (Figure 2).

Figure 2. HOMER Modeling Flow

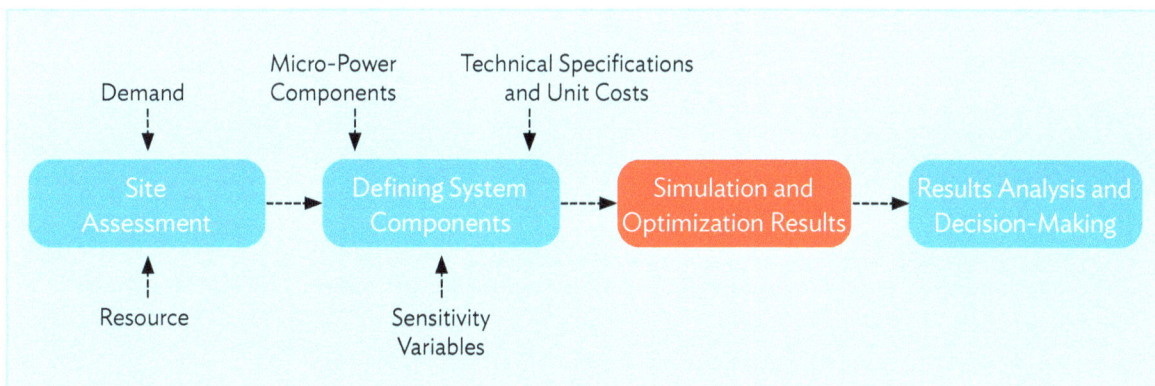

HOMER = Hybrid Optimization of Multiple Energy Resources.
Source: ADB.

Site assessment. Tapping available renewable energy resources and maximizing the use of energy produced contribute to the system's economic viability. Quantifying resources and making sound projections of electricity consumption are important to properly size and design the system.

(i) **Demand assessment**. A 24-hour load profile is the primary input for HOMER modeling. It indicates the amount of electricity that must be produced to ensure reliable service. A community's total energy demand includes requirements of (a) households for consumptive and productive uses of energy, (b) the production sector, and (c) community services (Shrestha and Acharya 2015). Historical load profiles will be absent in energy-deprived sites and the load profile may be constructed through the conduct of surveys or by referencing demand patterns in similar sites.

(ii) **Resource assessment**. Incorporating renewable energy into the system entails identifying which resources are available and analyzing if the levels are enough for power generation. Geospatial resource maps provide secondary information that may be used to identify which resources to further investigate. Most renewable energy resource maps are accessed from national or international databases. In the absence of credible secondary data, HOMER links to NREL and National Aeronautics and Space Administration (NASA) database to acquire solar irradiance and wind speed data that will be used in the modeling. In designing systems, on-site resource measurements are ideal since this will form the basis of significant investment decisions related to equipment and infrastructure.

Defining system components. Table 8 lists the types of components that HOMER can model, which include power generating equipment (renewable and dispatchable energy), energy storage, and converters. Default technical specifications and unit costs of each component are available in the HOMER library, but actual component data can be used for more precise simulations. Inputs for sensitivity analysis can likewise be defined.

Table 8. Micro-Power Components Modeled in HOMER

Renewable Energy	Dispatchable Energy	Energy Storage	Converters[a]
Solar PV Modules	Generators[b]	Batteries	Converters
Wind turbines	Grid	Hydrogen Storage	Electrolyzers[c]
Run-of-the-river hydro turbines	Boilers	Flywheels	

HOMER = Hybrid Optimization of Multiple Energy Resources, PV = photovoltaic.
Notes:
[a] Converts electrical energy into another form.
[b] Biogas and biomass are modeled under the generator component.
[c] Electrolyzers convert AC (alternating current) or DC (direct current) electricity into hydrogen via the electrolysis of water.
Source: ADB.

Simulation and optimization results. HOMER models how the selected components work together as a system. It simulates dispatch strategies for nonrenewable components and energy storage components, as well as prioritizes serving of loads. At the end of the simulation, it generates a table of technically feasible system configurations with performance metrics and system cost estimates. HOMER's optimization process ranks system configurations according to the lowest total net present cost by default, or the user's prescribed parameter.

Results analysis. HOMER eliminates the guesswork in the system design process and allows designers to investigate system performance in a short amount of time. The technical and economic parameters generated by HOMER's simulation and operation processes may be used as decision factors when selecting the optimal system configuration for the site. Some users may prefer a system with the lowest greenhouse gas (GHG) emissions over one that has the lowest net present cost, if the intention of the project is to transition to a lower carbon economy or access subsidies or grants that prescribe a GHG threshold. In isolated off-grid sites, it is critical to install systems with the least life cycle cost because margins are thin. Managing capital and operating costs will improve affordability and contribute to the sustainability of the operation.

Parameters that HOMER generates in its simulation process include the following:

Technical Parameters:

1. **Renewable penetration** (%) refers to the percentage of renewable energy production that supplies the load. Countries that are transitioning to low-carbon technologies or have renewable energy targets can use this metric to identify systems that utilize more renewable energy-based production. It is a better gauge to measure utilization of renewable energy resources compared to system capacities whose production may not necessarily be utilized fully by the load. Renewable energy penetration based on energy production should be distinguished from penetration based on capacity. High-capacity penetration of variable renewable energy sources will require tight control of the system operation, the use of energy storage, or enough reserve capacity from non-variable sources.

2. **Total fuel** (liter/year) indicates the volume of fuel that will be consumed by the system per year. Logistically challenged sites would benefit from low fuel requirements to reduce associated transportation and storage costs.

Economic Parameters:

1. **Total net present cost** represents the present value of all the costs the system incurs over its lifetime, less the present value of all the revenue it earns. Costs include capital costs, replacement costs, O&M costs, fuel costs, emissions penalties, and the costs of buying power from the grid. Revenues include salvage value and sales to an external grid (but does not include sales from the load it is serving).[6] A lower net present cost will redound to lower pass-on rates to end users.

---

[6] Revenues from the distributed grid is not included in the computation because it will be equal across all simulation options. All systems must supply the identified demand profile. On the other hand, sales to an external grid will happen only when there is excess production that will vary depending on dispatch strategies and other variables. For energy access mini-grids, connection to an external grid can happen when the national grid is extended to the area.

2. **Levelized cost of electricity** (LCOE) is the average cost per kWh of useful electrical energy produced by the system. To calculate the LCOE, HOMER divides the annualized cost of producing electricity (the total annualized cost minus the cost of serving the thermal load) by the total electric load served, using the following equation:

$$LCOE = \frac{C_{ann,tot} - C_{boiler} H_{served}}{E_{served}}$$

where:

$C_{ann,tot}$	=	total annualized cost of the system ($/year)
C_{boiler}	=	boiler marginal cost ($/kWh)
H_{served}	=	total thermal load served (kWh/year)
E_{served}	=	total electrical load served (kWh/year)

Environmental Parameter:

GHG emissions (kilogram/year) calculates system emissions that include levels of carbon dioxide, carbon monoxide, unburned hydrocarbons, particulate matter, sulfur dioxide, and nitrogen oxides. This parameter may be used to measure environmental impact when compared to business-as-usual systems.

5 Case Study—Cobrador Hybrid Solar Photovoltaic Mini-Grid

Policies and Regulations That Enable Distributed Electrification

The Energy for All Initiative extended its technical assistance services to the Philippines to pilot a renewable energy mini-grid hybrid project. The guide for deploying distributed renewable energy system was applied to demonstrate the project's technical and economic viability. The enabling policy and regulatory environment in the Philippines supported the implementation of the pilot, which may be replicated in other areas in the Philippines and other DMCs.

By law, the entire country is divided into 150 franchise areas that are assigned to distinct distribution utilities—electric cooperatives (ECs), private investor-owned utilities or local government unit-owned utilities.[7] Each of these entities has the sole right to distribute electricity within their franchise area, unless this responsibility is waived to a third party for a given period. The distribution utilities are expected to provide energy access to all households within their franchise areas.

Two policies grant distribution utilities the unique power to participate in both energy distribution and generation—the Electric Power Industry Reform Act and National Electrification Administration Reform Act.

1. **Republic Act (RA) 9136,** also known as the **Electric Power Industry Reform Act (EPIRA) of 2001** restructured the energy sector and mandated the privatization and deregulation of the industry. The previously vertically integrated National Power Corporation was unbundled into four sectors: generation, transmission, distribution, and supply. Other policies include the (a) introduction of competition in the generation sector through the creation of the electricity spot market, (b) change from government to private ownership of generation and transmission assets, and (c) extension of regulatory framework to cover private sector-led activities in the electricity sector.

2. **RA 10531,** also known as the **National Electrification Administration (NEA) Reform Act of 2013,** aims to empower and strengthen the NEA to pursue the government's rural electrification program through ECs. The ECs will act as NEA's implementing arm for rural areas, which includes missionary or economically unviable areas. Furthermore, RA 10531 allows ECs to

   (i) Construct, acquire, own, operate, and maintain electric sub-transmission and distribution lines in publicly owned lands and public thoroughfares; and
   (ii) Engage in power generation within its franchise area through the (a) construction of an embedded generating facility, and (b) acquisition of an existing privately owned generation

---

[7] Philippine Department of Energy (DOE). *Distribution Development Plan 2016–2025.* https://www.doe.gov.ph/sites/default/files/pdf/electric_power/ddp_2016-2025_as_of_may_3_2018_edited_page_37.pdf; and Philippine DOE. Distribution Utility Profile. https://www.doe.gov.ph/duprofile?title=&field_du_group_value=&field_du_region_value

facility, government-owned generating facility in the main grid, and areas currently being powered by the National Power Corporation's Small Power Utilities Group (NPC-SPUG).[8]

Distribution utilities that are unable to fully electrify their franchise area due to economic or technical limitations may waive their right to provide service to these sites to qualified third parties (QTPs). New power producers (NPPs) take over the provision of electricity in missionary areas that are operated by NPC-SPUG. The QTP and NPP mechanisms are the pathways where the private sector may participate in rural electrification.

1. **A qualified third party (QTP)** is a private entity that carries out missionary electrification functions in villages and townships that have been waived by a distribution utility. A QTP must secure its own power supply, and construct and operate the distribution network in the area.

2. **New power producers (NPPs)** can take over larger NPC-SPUG sites through a competitive selection process either through outright purchase, or lease of existing SPUG assets and/or installation of new power generation facilities. This allows NPC-SPUG to utilize its limited resources among a smaller client base, or to finance the expansion of its services to unserved missionary sites.

3. **QTPs** and **NPPs** are eligible for a subsidy from the national government called the Universal Charge for Missionary Electrification (UCME). The UCME allows private companies to recover the full cost of generation in off-grid areas since they charge a discounted electricity tariff in these areas. The government's budget for the UCME is replenished periodically through a non-bypass fee collected from all residential, commercial, and industrial electricity payments throughout the country, as mandated by law.

Apart from EPIRA and NEA Reform Act, Republic Act 9513 or the Renewable Energy (RE) Act of 2018 further enhances the cost competitiveness of electrification solutions that utilize renewable energy technologies. The RE Act aims to reduce the country's dependency on imported fossil fuels and ensure energy security by accelerating the exploration and development of renewable energy resources, promoting its efficient and cost-effective commercial application and encouraging its use for balancing the goals of economic growth, including protection of health and the environment. The RE Act offers fiscal and non-fiscal incentives to private companies that participate in renewable energy generation.

Electrification Targets of the Philippine Government

As of 31 December 2016, the Philippine government extended modern energy services to 90% of its population.[9] This leaves more than 2.1 million households without access to electricity. Majority of the remaining unelectrified households reside in remote and off-grid areas where grid extension is not economically justifiable.

---

8   EPIRA mandated the NPC-SPUG to lead the provision of power generation and electricity distribution services to areas that are not connected to the main transmission system. Such areas are referred to as missionary areas that are mostly remote, isolated, and too costly to connect to the grid.
9   International Energy Agency 2017.

NPC-SPUG operates 288 missionary sites in the country (Table 9). These have been identified and classified according to their viability for private sector takeover.[10] Power supply in missionary areas is dominated by oil-based generation. SPUG operates 274 oil-based power plants with a total rated capacity of 215.5 MW and the 1.8 MW Balongbong Hydroelectric Power Plant in Catanduanes (NPC-SPUG 2017). Given the heavy dependence on diesel and bunker C fuel, the operating cost in SPUG sites is significantly influenced by oil price movements. Moreover, the cost of transporting and storing fuel in geographically challenging sites adds to the final cost of electrification in these areas. Consequently, subsidy burden to the UCME increases as operation in missionary areas strive to catch up to the growing demand at increasing operating costs.

Table 9. Delivery of Electricity Services in Missionary Areas

Cluster	Number of Areas	Average Service Hours	Peak Demand (MW)	Gross Generation (GWh)
Large	16	24	173.10	942.65
Medium	21	22	23.90	104.41
Small A	63	10	9.80	20.63
Small B	32	7	0.77	0.91
PRES Mini-Grids[a]	153	5	1.00	1.27
QTP Mini-Grids	3[b]	24	0.78	4.30

GWh = gigawatt-hour, MW = megawatt, PRES = Philippine Rural Electrification System, QTP = qualified third party

Notes:

a   PRES mini-grids were financed by concessional and commercial loans through the French-Philippine protocol. It consists of distribution of solar home systems and small generation sets by the National Power Corporation's Small Power Utilities Group.

b   One more QTP commenced operation in April 2018, performance data are not yet available.

Source: Philippine Department of Energy. *Missionary Electrification Development Plan 2016–2020.* https://www.doe.gov.ph/sites/default/files/pdf/electric_power/medp_2016-2020.pdf.

The 2016–2030 Philippine Energy Plan (PEP) has set the target for the total electrification of the country: (i) 90% household electrification level by 2017, (ii) total household electrification by 2022, and (iii) continuing implementation of NEA's *sitio* electrification program.[11] While not articulated directly, the spirit of the PEP aims to provide the highest level of electrification possible to its citizens. Given the prevalent use of diesel generators in missionary areas, Energy for All and NEA decided to pilot the solar PV–diesel hybrid mini-grid to provide Tier 5 access to Cobrador Island.

---

10   Philippine DOE. *Missionary Electrification Development Plan 2016–2020.* https://www.doe.gov.ph/sites/default/files/pdf/electric_power/medp_2016-2020.pdf

11   *Sitio* refers to an administrative unit at the local level that is traditionally used to name the location of remote cluster of households living outside the barangay (village) proper. The government has no official definition (in terms of geographical boundaries) and database of *sitios* (DOE).

Rationale and Objectives of the Pilot Project

Energy for All partnered with the ROMELCO, which has experience in operating renewable energy projects to pilot test a solar PV–diesel hybid mini-grid in Cobrador Island in Romblon province. ROMELCO was operating a 15-kW generator set in Cobrador Island that provided 8 hours of service at a Tier 3 level of access to 59% of the households. In line with the government's aim of total electrification, ROMELCO committed to provide reliable 24-hour electricity service (Tier 5) to all end users in Cobrador as it has done in other islands within its franchise area.

The implementing organization is a crucial factor to ensure project sustainability. ROMELCO earned its expertise in renewable energy when it developed the Cantingas micro-hydropower plant. It is the first renewable energy distributed generation project solely developed by an electric cooperative (EC) that aimed to offset diesel consumption in the mini-grid of Sibuyan Island, also in Romblon province. ROMELCO established a subsidiary called the Cantingas Micro-Hydropower Corporation to operate and maintain the facility.

Personnel under the Cantingas Micro-Hydropower Corporation were assigned to also operate and maintain the solar PV–diesel hybrid plant in Cobrador Island. Their technical expertise, operational experience, and the relatively minimal oversight required for the hydropower power plant were important factors in this decision. These personnel received additional training on solar PV-hybrid technology operation from BJ Power, the Republic of Korea-based engineering, procurement, and construction (EPC) contractor assigned by KEA for the project. Under its contract, BJ Power will provide technical support to ROMELCO for 3 years to resolve technical concerns and contribute in building staff capacity to run and maintain the system.

The pilot project was implemented under a letter of agreement signed among ADB, NEA, KEA, and ROMELCO. In line with the government's goal of total electrification, the pilot project aims to promote distributed renewable energy solutions that provide affordable, reliable, and sustainable electricity, and to increase Cobrador Island's access level from Tier 3 (medium power) to Tier 5 (high power).

Energy Demand and Supply Characteristics of Cobrador Island

Cobrador Island is one of the island barangays of Romblon municipality in Romblon province, Philippines.[12] As of 2013, 138 out of 234 households or approximately 59% of the local population were connected to the diesel mini-grid. As electricity services were only available 8 hours per day, grid-connected households still used kerosene for lighting and dry cell batteries for radio and other appliances during hours when the generator set (genset) was not operating. Others prefer to use kerosene for lighting because of the high electricity tariff. About 100 households rely on kerosene for light, and 38 households had either solar home systems or solar lanterns.

ROMELCO owns and operates the 15-kW diesel genset and mini-grid that supplies electricity to Cobrador Island. The diesel genset operated for only 8 hours a day, that is, 2 hours in the morning (4:00 a.m.–6:00 a.m.) and 6 hours in the evening (5:00 p.m.–11:00 p.m.). A single-phase distribution line was constructed covering one third of the island. Peak demand was 10 kW in 2013 (Table 10).

---

[12]   A barangay means a village and is the basic political unit in the Philippines.

ROMELCO charged ₱30/kWh ($0.60) for electricity in the island, although according to ROMELCO, the cost of generation was about double this amount.

As Cobrador Island is mostly residential, electricity demand peaks during the evening with a relatively low load factor, as shown in (Figure 3). Peak demand was 10 kW with daily consumption of about 30 kWh among the grid-connected households. This means that the average monthly consumption per household was only 6.52 kWh, much lower than the average monthly consumption of all ROMELCO consumers that is 56.46 kWh (ADB, NEA, KEA 2015). This lower consumption may be attributed to the limited 8 hours of electricity supply, few commercial and industrial activities, and higher tariff in Cobrador Island as compared to the main island of Romblon.

Figure 3. Cobrador Island 8-Hour Load Profile, 2013

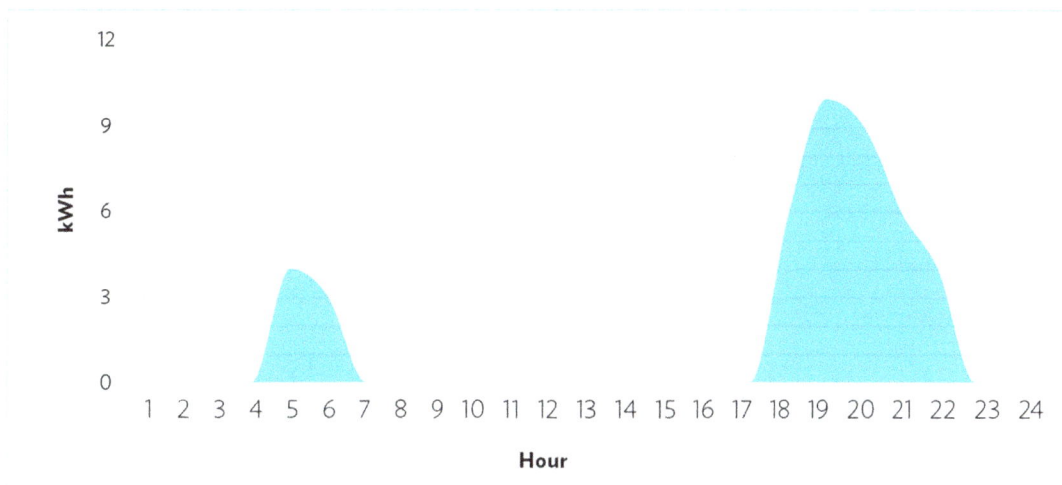

kWh = kilowatt-hour

Source: ADB, Korea Energy Agency, and National Electrification Administration. 2015. Hybridizing Existing Diesel Power Plants with Renewable Energy: A Feasibility Study. Philippines. Unpublished.

Table 10. Cobrador Island Electricity Status, 2013

Location	Population (Number of HHs)	Number of HHs Energized	Average Daily Demand	Peak Demand	Operating Hours	Diesel Cost	Diesel Generator Set Capacity
Cobrador Island, Romblon province	983 (234 HHs)	138 (59%)	30.07 kWh/day	10 kW	8 Hours	$1/L	15 kW

HH = household, kW = kilowatt, kWh = kilowatt-hour, L = liter.

Source: ADB, Korea Energy Agency, and National Electrification Administration. 2015. Feasibility Study: Hybridizing Existing Diesel Power Plants with Renewable Energy. Philippines. Unpublished.

Cobrador Island's future electricity demand was projected from consumption data of existing consumers (Table 10) and electricity sales data (Table 12), and referenced with load patterns of similar islands with 24-hour access. ROMELCO forecasted the potential electricity demand of different consumer sectors using the 2013 consumption data of existing customers as baseline. Electricity was used primarily for lighting and small appliances, and none for productive use due to the limited power supply. Only informal, small-scale commercial activity by households, such as village stores, were present.

Demand from a large-load household is expected by 2021. The electricity that will be used by the powerhouse was also included in the projections. Table 11 shows the historical and forecasted load profile of each consumer sector.

Table 11. Forecasted Daily Load per Customer Sector (kWh/day)

Classification	Historical Load 2013	Forecasted Load 2015	2018	2021
Household/Residential				
Average Household	38.50	79.22	125.95	166.80
Large Load Household	0.00	0.00	0.00	23.00
Subtotal Household/Residential	38.50	79.22	125.95	189.80
Government and Community Buildings and Services				
Elementary School	–	3.17	3.17	5.00
Barangay Hall	–	0.05	0.05	2.00
Barangay Outpost	–	0.10	0.10	0.10
Day Care or Health Center	–	0.70	0.70	2.00
Churches	–	1.80	1.80	3.00
Streetlighting	1.60	2.80	2.80	2.80
Subtotal Government and Community	1.60	8.62	8.62	14.90
Powerhouse				
Air Conditioner	0.00	9.00	9.00	9.00
House Load	1.50	3.00	3.00	3.00
Subtotal Powerhouse	1.50	12.00	12.00	12.00
Overall Total	**41.60**	**99.84**	**146.57**	**216.70**

– = data not available, kWh = kilowatt-hour.
Source: ADB, Korea Energy Agency, and National Electrification Administration. 2015. Feasibility Study: Hybridizing Existing Diesel Power Plants with Renewable Energy. Philippines. Unpublished.

Cobrador Island's electricity sales data in 2010–2013 (Table 12) was also used as reference for forecasting the demand of the mini-grid. During this period, only 8 hours of electricity services or a Tier 3 level of access was provided. The forecasted load demand, as presented in Table 12, shows increasing demand up to year 2021 where peak load will reach 21 kW and daily demand 181 kWh.

Table 12. Historical 8-Hour Demand and Forecasted 24-Hour Demand of Cobrador Island

Item	Historical Demand (Tier 3)				Forecasted Demand (Tier 5)			
	2010	2011	2012	2013	2015	2017	2019	2021
Operating Hours	8	8	8	8	24	24	24	24
Number of Customers	32	61	92	138	170	211	247	278
Energy Sales (MWh/year)	3.98	5.26	7.22	8.89	36.08	45.92	55.91	65.96
Peak Demand (kW)	6	7	8	10	12	15	18	21
Daily Demand (kWh/day)	10.90	14.41	19.78	24.36	99.00	125.80	153.19	181.00
Daily Demand per Customer (kWh/customer/day)	0.341	0.236	0.215	0.203	0.582	0.596	0.615	0.651

kW= kilowatt, kWh = kilowatt-hour, MWh = megawatt-hour.
Source: ADB, Korea Energy Agency, and National Electrification Administration. 2015. Feasibility Study: Hybridizing Existing Diesel Power Plants with Renewable Energy. Philippines. Unpublished.

From 2010 to 2013, the number of customers in Cobrador Island tripled to 138, but daily consumption per customer steadily declined from 0.34 kWh to 0.20 kWh, a 40% reduction (Table 12). With increasing number of connections, the limited production of the available 15-kW generator is shared by more households, effectively reducing consumption per connection. Limited availability of diesel in the island further constrained energy production.

Figure 4 shows that with Tier 5 energy access, the average daily demand can increase over time even with growing number of customers. Enhancing power generation is projected to increase daily household consumption to 0.65 kWh, with affordability and service reliability as the primary drivers of growth. Increase in electricity consumption at a system level will be caused by (i) increased use of appliances, (ii) establishment of small enterprises and microenterprises, (iii) lower tariffs over time, and (iv) additional households that connect to the mini-grid.

Figure 4. Tier 3 and Tier 5 Average Daily Demand per Customer

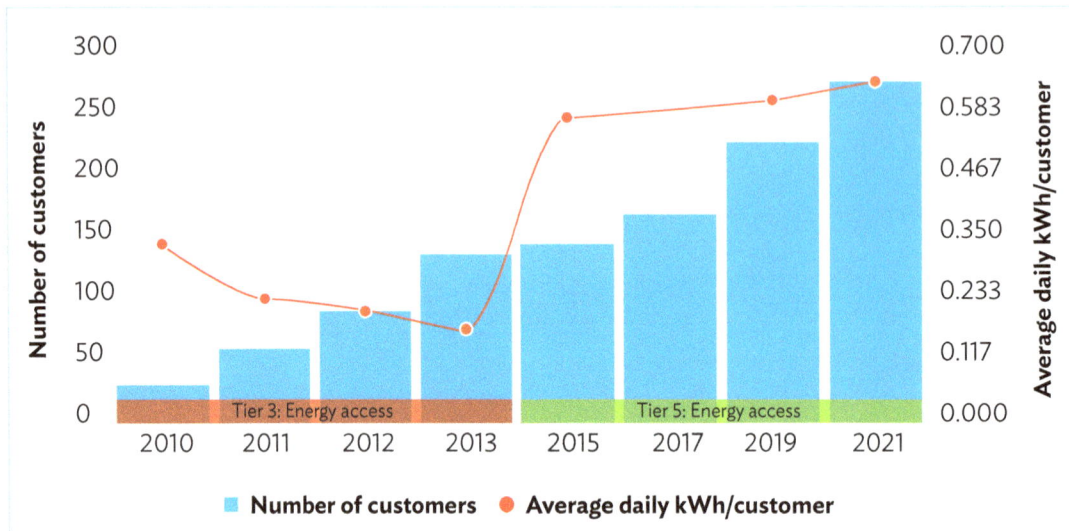

kWh = kilowatt-hour.
Source: ADB.

To meet the increase in demand without disrupting the quality of service, some components of the system have been oversized. The design of the pilot project factored in a 30% higher capacity for energy storage and all wiring specifications. These provisions allow additional generation equipment to be added in the future, without requiring additional investment on the plant infrastructure. Overall, the pilot project was designed to offer Tier 5 electrification to the forecasted demand in 2015, when it will be operational.

Renewable Energy Supply Analysis

Solar energy is the most abundant renewable energy resources in Cobrador Island. According to the US NREL data set, average global horizontal irradiation in Cobrador was 4.58 kWh/square meter (m²)/day (Figure 5). Wind potential was deemed inadequate at the 10-meter altitude required by the 10 kW turbine that corresponded to the energy demand.[13] No hydropower resources were found in Cobrador that can be used for energy generation. Residues from agriculture activity were found to be insufficient to support biomass power generation.

---

[13] The wind speed indicator shows that the effective wind speed at a 10m altitude is 4.9 meters per second, based on the 2003 wind speed table of the Danish Wind Power Association.

Figure 5. Global Horizontal Irradiation of the Philippines and Cobrador Island

kWh = kilowatt-hour, m^2 = square meter.

Note: Global horizontal irradiation is in kWh/m^2/year.

Sources: World Bank Group. 2016. Global Solar Atlas. https://globalsolaratlas.info (accessed March 2019); ADB, Korea Energy Agency, and National Electrification Administration. 2015. Feasibility Study: Hybridizing Existing Diesel Power Plants with Renewable Energy. Philippines. Unpublished.

Selection of System Configuration through HOMER Simulation

Preliminary assessment of the renewable energy geospatial maps and secondary information reveal that solar energy has the highest potential for power generation for Cobrador among the various renewable energy resources. The four potential micro-power configurations are the following:

(i) **Option A: 15 kW diesel capacity + additional capacity.** The projected demand may be supplied by increasing the capacity of the existing diesel generator set.

(ii) **Option B: Solar PV + ESS.** The mini-grid may be supplied by 100% renewable energy by utilizing solar power produced in daytime and drawing stored solar energy from the batteries at night.

(iii) **Option C: Solar PV + Diesel.** Power generated by the solar PV modules may be used at daytime while the generator set will supply the demand at night.

(iv) **Option D: 15 kW diesel + Solar PV + ESS.** Solar PV may be used to generate power on demand, charge the ESS with excess production, and use the stored power at night. In this configuration, the diesel genset will act as a back-up when solar energy is limited.

HOMER was used to find the least-cost option among the four potential configurations listed above (among many others). The forecasted load profile for the expected year of operation (2015) was used as the required amount of power that must be supplied by the system. It incorporates conservative estimates on suppressed demand.

The HOMER modeling results show possible system configurations that can supply the demand, including the four options being considered (Table 13). Performance indicators, such as fuel consumption and renewable energy penetration are indicated among other metrics.

Table 13. HOMER Optimization Results for Cobrador Island

								Optimization Results						
	Export...							Left Double Click on a particular system to see its detailed Simulation Results.						
	Architecture								Cost				System	
	⚠	☀	🏭	🔋	📈	PV (kW)	GenEx (kW)	ESS_LG	Convert-er (kW)	Dispatch	COE ($)	NPC ($)	Operating Cost ($/yr)	Initial Capital ($)	Ren Frac (%)	Total Fuel (L/yr)
Option D	⚠	☀	🏭	🔋	📈	30.0	15.0	720	25.0	CC	$0.81	$333,633	$13,023	$184,260	80.50	2,346
Option B		☀		🔋	📈	60.0	-	900	25.0	CC	$0.92	$378,386	$9,737	$266,700	100.00	0
			🏭	🔋	📈	-	15.0	720	25.0	CC	$1.12	$464,896	$29,960	$121,260	0.00	14,885
Option C	⚠	☀	🏭		📈	30.0	15.0	-	25.0	CC	$1.22	$504,582	$36,276	$88,500	1.43	16,329
Option A			🏭			-	15.0	-	-	CC	$1.27	$527,209	$45,572	$4,500	0.00	22,330

CC = cycle charging, COE = levelized cost of electricity, ESS_LG = energy storage system, GenEx = generator set, HOMER = Hybrid Optimization of Multiple Energy Resources, kW = kilowatt, L = liter, NPC = net present cost, PV = photovoltaic, Ren Frac = renewable fraction, yr = year.

Source: ADB.

Analysis of the simulation results (Table 14) points to Option D, which is the solar PV–diesel hybrid with energy storage, as the solution with the least-cost of energy to supply the Cobrador demand over the project life of 25 years. In this simulation, the costs are associated only with the installation and operation of the hybrid power system and does not include external costs such as access roads and taxes.

HOMER's simulation calculated that the system can produce 50,300 kWh of electricity annually, where the solar PV contributes 86% of the power output (Figure 6). The system is expected to meet and exceed by 17% the conservative forecast consumption of 99 kWh/day or 36,135 kWh/year. DC/AC conversion loss is estimated at 14,000 kWh/year. The renewable fraction refers to the percentage of power produced from renewable energy sources that is consumed by the load, which is at 80% for this system. The bottom graph depicts the high solar PV production peaking during the summer months of April and May. Low power output from the generator indicates low consumption of diesel fuel while ensuring that power is enough to supply the demand.

Table 14. Analysis of Simulation and Optimization Results

Options	LCOE ($)	NPC ($)	Operating Cost ($/year)	Initial Capital ($)	Renewable Fraction (%)	Total Fuel (L/year)	CO$_2$ Emissions (kg/year)
	1.27	$527,209	$45,572	$4,500	0	22,330	58,800
A. Pure Diesel 15 kW Diesel Genset							

Option A has the highest NPC among all other options contributed by high O&M and fuel costs. The existing 15kW diesel genset can technically supply the demand of the site. However, this simulation did not include equipment downtime and fuel availability that will affect reliability of power supply. Without renewable energy component, this option generates the most CO$_2$ emissions.

Options	LCOE ($)	NPC ($)	Operating Cost ($/year)	Initial Capital ($)	Renewable Fraction (%)	Total Fuel (L/year)	CO$_2$ Emissions (kg/year)
B. Solar and Storage 60 kW Solar PV 215 kWh ESS (900 cells) 25 kW Converter	0.92	$378,386	$9,737	$266,700	100	0	0

Option B has the second lowest NPC among the scenarios. It requires larger Solar PV capacity to be able to feed the load as well as charge the batteries for nighttime use. While this system incurs no fuel costs, the initial capital cost is highest among all the options because of the large sizes of solar PV and ESS required to supply the demand.

Options	LCOE ($)	NPC ($)	Operating Cost ($/year)	Initial Capital ($)	Renewable Fraction (%)	Total Fuel (L/year)	CO$_2$ Emissions (kg/year)
	1.22	$504,582	$36,276	$88,500	1.43	16,329	43,000
C. Solar and Diesel 30 kW Solar PV 15 kW Diesel Genset 25 kW Converter							

The load is fed by the solar PV when solar resources are available at daytime, while the diesel genset takes over production at night. However, Cobrador's load is low during the day generating surplus solar power that may affect the stability of the grid. The load cannot maximize solar PV power production without any energy storage system. As a result, there is minimal penetration of renewable energy to the load. Fuel consumption is high given that only the diesel genset will supply peak demand at night.

Options	LCOE ($)	NPC ($)	Operating Cost ($/year)	Initial Capital ($)	Renewable Fraction (%)	Total Fuel (L/year)	CO$_2$ Emissions (kg/year)
D. Solar and Diesel with Storage 30 kW Solar PV 15 kW Diesel Genset 172 kWh ESS (720 cells) 25 kW Converter	0.81	$333,633	$13,023	$184,260	80.5	2,346	6,179

This option has the lowest NPC among all the other options. Estimated renewable energy penetration is respectably high with low CO$_2$ emissions. In this configuration, solar PV generation feeds the grid and charges the battery. The diesel genset is only activated when solar PV production and battery charge is low.

CO$_2$ = carbon dioxide, ESS = energy storage system, genset = generator set, kg = kilogram, kW = kilowatt, kWh = kilowatt-hour, L = liter, LCOE = levelized cost of electricity, NPC = net present cost, O&M = operation and maintenance, PV = photovoltaic.
Source: ADB.

Figure 6. Simulated Levels of Electricity Production

Production	kWh/yr	%		Consumption	kWh/yr	%		Quantity	kWh/yr	%		Quantity	Value
PV	43,256	86.0		AC Primary Load	36,135	100		Excess Electricity	8,303	16.5		Renewable Fraction	80.5
Generator 1	7,058	14.0		DC Primary Load	0	0		Unmet Electric Load	0	0		Max. Renew. Penetration	1,007
Total	50,313	100		Deferrable Load	0	0		Capacity Shortage	0	0			
				Total	36,135	100							

Monthly Average Electric Production

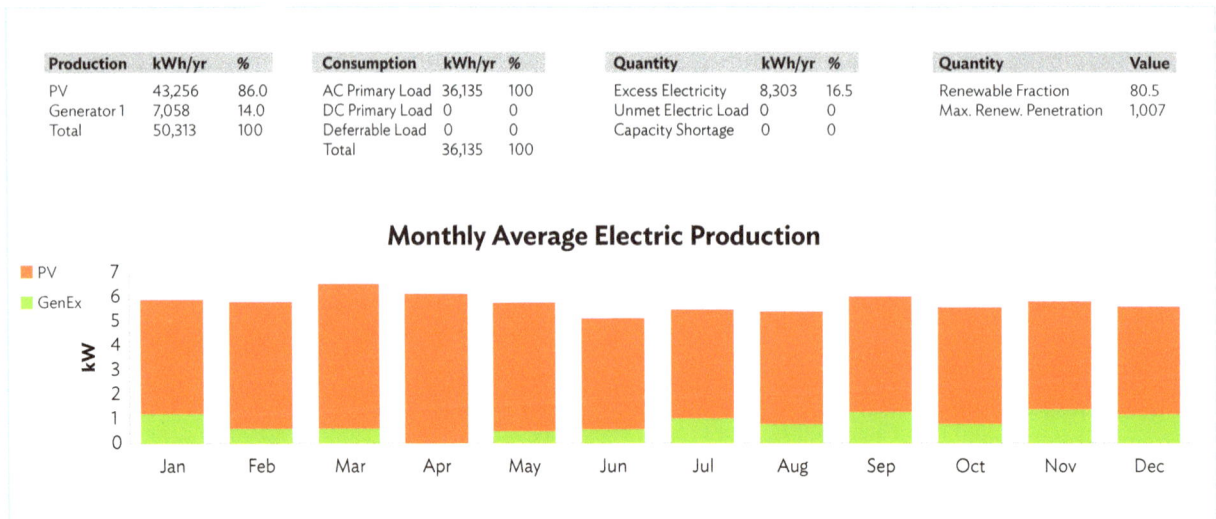

AC = alternating current, DC = direct current, GenEx = generator set, kW = kilowatt, kWh = kilowatt hour, PV = photovoltaic, yr = year.

Source: ADB.

HOMER's time series simulation shows how the various power components work together as a system to supply the demand. Figure 7 shows how the load is mostly supplied by the inverter's output that channels power produced from solar PV or from the batteries. The generator steps in as soon as the ESS reaches its minimum state of charge (SOC) that was set at 20%. It operates to supply the demand, and ramps up to charge the ESS.

Figure 7. Simulation of the System's Operation

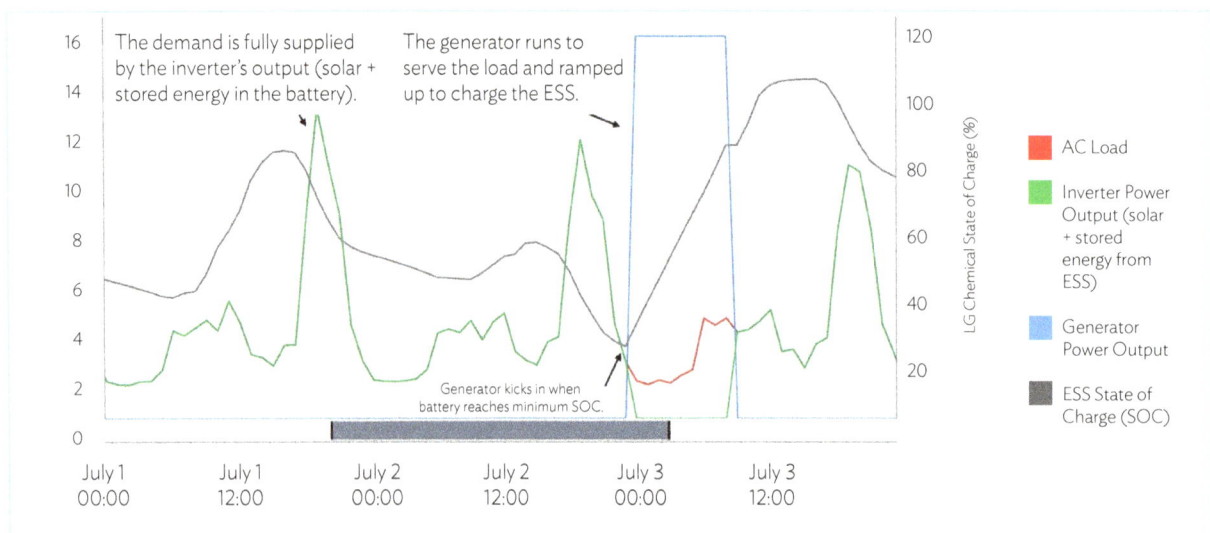

AC = alternating current, ESS = energy storage system, SOC = state of charge.

Source: ADB.

Final Configuration of the Micro-Power System

The solar PV–diesel–storage hybrid system was found to be the least-cost configuration for Cobrador. The final configuration of the pilot micro-power plant is shown in Figure 8. Two power generation sources feed Cobrador's AC load. Energy generated by the PV modules supply the load through the AC/DC inverter. Excess energy produced by the PV panels is stored in the energy storage system (ESS). Conversely, if the energy supplied by the PV panels is not enough to meet the load, then the system will go into a decision mode and determine which component (batteries or diesel genset) has priority to supply energy based on the following conditions:

(i)   The ESS will be used, if the SOC of the battery is greater than the set minimum SOC.
(ii) The diesel genset will be activated to supply the load and charge the ESS, if the solar PV modules produce limited energy and the battery is at its minimum SOC.

Figure 8. Schematic Diagram of the Solar PV–Diesel–ESS Hybrid System

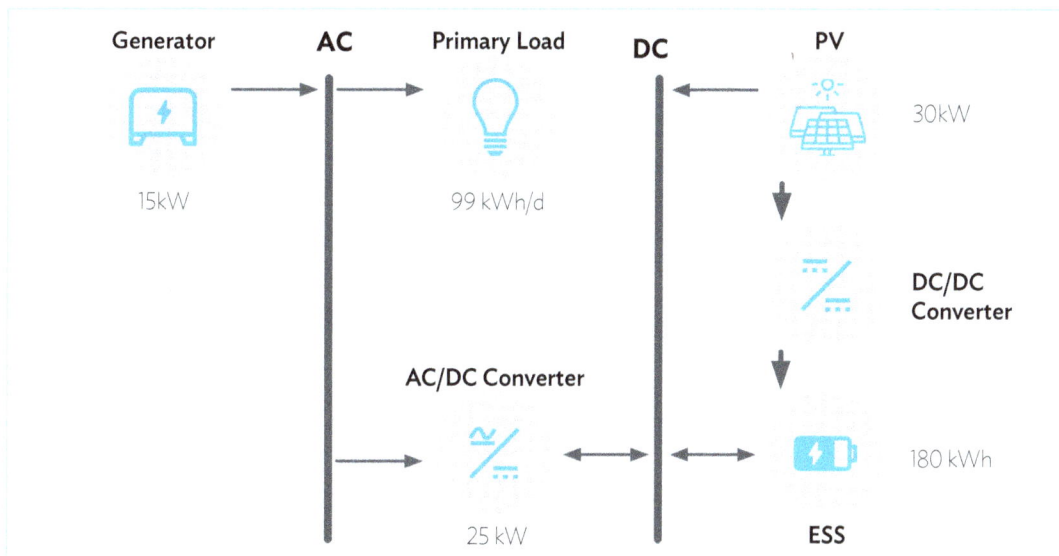

AC = alternating current, d = day, DC = direct current, ESS = energy storage system, kW = kilowatt, kWh = kilowatt-hour, PV = photovoltaic.
Source: ADB.

The DC/DC converter is a component outside of HOMER modeling and was added as an engineering design decision. This converter reduces losses from storing energy at different voltages. The availability of specific sizes of components, as well as the budget, are factors that also influence the system's final configuration.

The system runs on cycle charging scheme where whenever the generator is operated to supply the load, its operation is ramped to charge the battery to the maximum extent possible. This strategy adds more energy to the battery and makes it more likely that the generator can be turned off during future periods of low load. Further, running generators at higher capacity contributes to its efficiency and ensures its proper operation.

Technical Performance of the Cobrador Hybrid Solar PV Power Plant

The Cobrador hybrid power plant was commissioned in March 2016. The facility has two main power generating sources, 30-kW of solar PV and 15-kW diesel generator, and includes a 180-kWh lithium ESS. The whole system is managed by a 30-kW power control system that governs dispatch of electricity from the system's power sources (solar PV, diesel genset, ESS). The powerhouse is a multi-functional two-story structure with four rooms (100 m² per floor) situated 20 m above seashore and adjacent to the cluster of houses in the community. Solar PV panels are installed on the rooftop that consist of 6 arrays, each containing 18 modules, and generates a maximum of 5.4 kW per array.

Powerhouse with Solar Photovoltaic Modules Installed at the Rooftop. The hybrid solar photovoltaic power plant is providing 24/7 electricity to the remote island of Cobrador in the Philippines (photo by Chrisanto George G. Quintana for Asian Development Bank).

Personnel were trained to operate and perform routine maintenance activities as well as troubleshoot minor technical problems. A remote monitoring system is in place to track performance and alert when the system is not functioning optimally. The EPC has a 3-year commitment to provide technical advice to ROMELCO and to perform annual on-site system checks.

Table 15 presents the capital costs of the hybrid system that totaled $416,500. The project was financed by contributions from ADB, KEA, and ROMELCO (Table 16). ADB financed the procurement of the lithium-ion energy storage system (180 kWh) on grant basis. KEA provided grant funding for the hybrid system design, procurement, and delivery of solar PV system components, as well as installation and commissioning. ROMELCO acquired a loan from NEA to cover the cost of constructing the powerhouse, access roads, transport of equipment, local fees, and importation taxes.

Table 15. System Cost

Item	Size	Cost ($)	Percent (%)
PV panels and support structure	30 kW	100,000	24.0
Energy storage system (lithium-ion battery)	180 kWh	106,500	25.6
Power converter system	30 kW	50,000	12.0
Diesel generator set	15 kW	10,000	2.4
Power house (including civil works, access roads, logistics, and other miscellaneous costs but not include any MV or LV grid)[a]	2-storey with 300 m^2	150,000	36.0
Total		**416,500**	**100.0**

ESS = energy storage system, kW = kilowatt, kWh = kilowatt-hour, LV = low voltage, m^2 = square meter, MV = medium voltage, PV = photovoltaic.

[a] The power house is a multi-functional building that will be used for training and transient housing in addition to housing the diesel generator set, the ESS, and the control room. The rooftop serves as the platform for the solar PV panels.

Source: ADB, Korea Energy Agency, and National Electrification Administration. 2015. Feasibility Study: Hybridizing Existing Diesel Power Plants with Renewable Energy. Unpublished.

Table 16. Breakdown of Financing of the Hybrid System

Item	Amount ($)	Percent (%)
Asian Development Bank	83,500	20.0
Korea Energy Agency	250,000	60.0
Romblon Electric Cooperative	83,000	20.0
Total	**416,500**	**100.0**

Source: ADB, Korea Energy Agency, and National Electrification Administration. 2015. Feasibility Study: Hybridizing Existing Diesel Power Plants with Renewable Energy. Unpublished.

ROMELCO charges a tariff rate ($0.30/kWh) that is 50% lower than the original rate ($0.60/kWh). This proved to be a strong driver for increased connections as well as demand growth. The rapid increase in consumption resulted in robust revenues that are sufficient to cover operating and maintenance costs, as well as repay its amortization to NEA.

Power demand increased steadily since the system's commissioning in March 2016. It peaked in May 2017 at 6,553 kWh (Figure 9). This increase in consumption can be attributed to the abrupt introduction of electric appliances such as TVs, refrigerators, and electric fans when the 24-hour electricity service became available. Moreover, the number of households connected to the mini-grid increased from the original 138 households to 260 (100% of the households). The average daily system demand grew to 200 kWh/day, which is the forecasted daily demand in 2021.

Even the daily load profile exhibited new daytime consumption peaks reflecting the change in electricity use behavior. In 2016, the daytime demand was relatively flat and peaked at night between 7:00 p.m. and 8:00 p.m. However, by 2017 demand also increased between 12 noon and 2:00 p.m. with peak load of 20 kW occurring at 8:00 p.m. (Figure 10).

Unexpected rapid demand growth and change in consumption patterns strained power generation of the solar PV-hybrid facility. While the system can supply up to 220 kWh/day when there is high solar radiation, solar PV cannot generate enough electricity to meet the demand during the rainy season. Solar irradiation is not sufficient to fully charge the battery while supplying the grid at the same time. ROMELCO therefore decided that from June to September, the hybrid system would be shut off from 6:00 a.m. to 12 noon to allow proper charging of the ESS. As a result, monthly power consumption decreased from 6,500 kWh in May to 5,700 kWh in June and 5,000 kWh in September. The average daily demand from June to September is about 150~170 kWh/day per household. In December 2017, ROMELCO added another 15 kW diesel into the system and small capacities of solar PV to augment supply and resume 24 hours service.

Apart from the need to increase the capacity of the system as a result of the high demand, other technical challenges that have been encountered by the hybrid facility include the following:

1. Corrosion on some parts of the control system which was resolved by encasing the equipment.

2. High temperature on the surface of the solar PV that affected solar energy production. The panels were doused with water everyday to bring down the temperature.

3. High temperature in the control room, especially during summer months, that can potentially affect the life of the equipment. ROMELCO installed an air conditioner in the control room to maintain optimum temperature.

4. To extend or ensure the optimal life of the hybrid system, particularly the ESS, which is costly, a new dispatch strategy was employed. The diesel generator was run first during peak hours (nighttime) instead of using the batteries' power output. This will extend the life of the batteries since it prevents discharging at high current that happens when the load is high.

Figure 9. Monthly Power Demand of the Installed Hybrid System

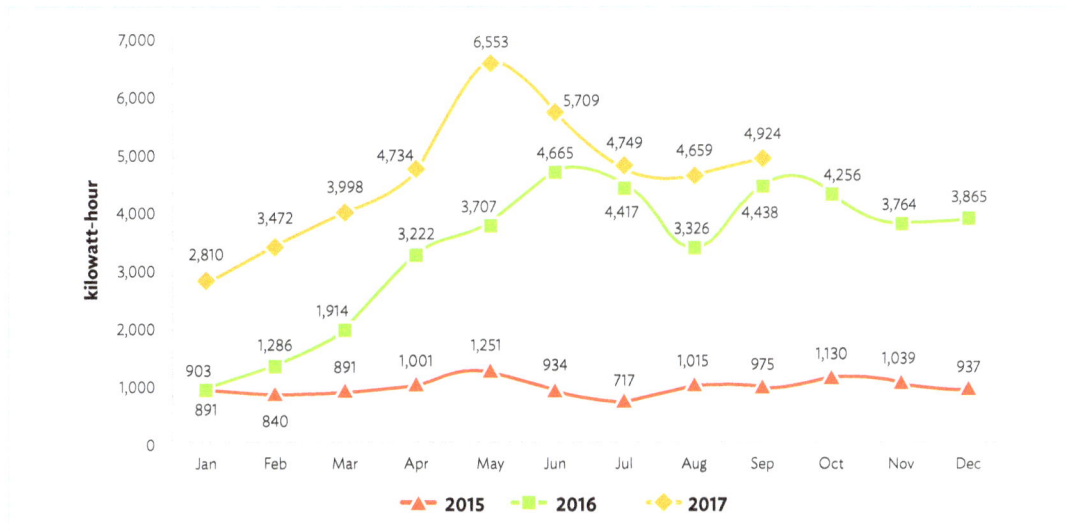

Source: Romblon Electric Cooperative.

Figure 10. Cobrador Island Daily Load Pattern Post-Commissioning of the Hybrid Plant

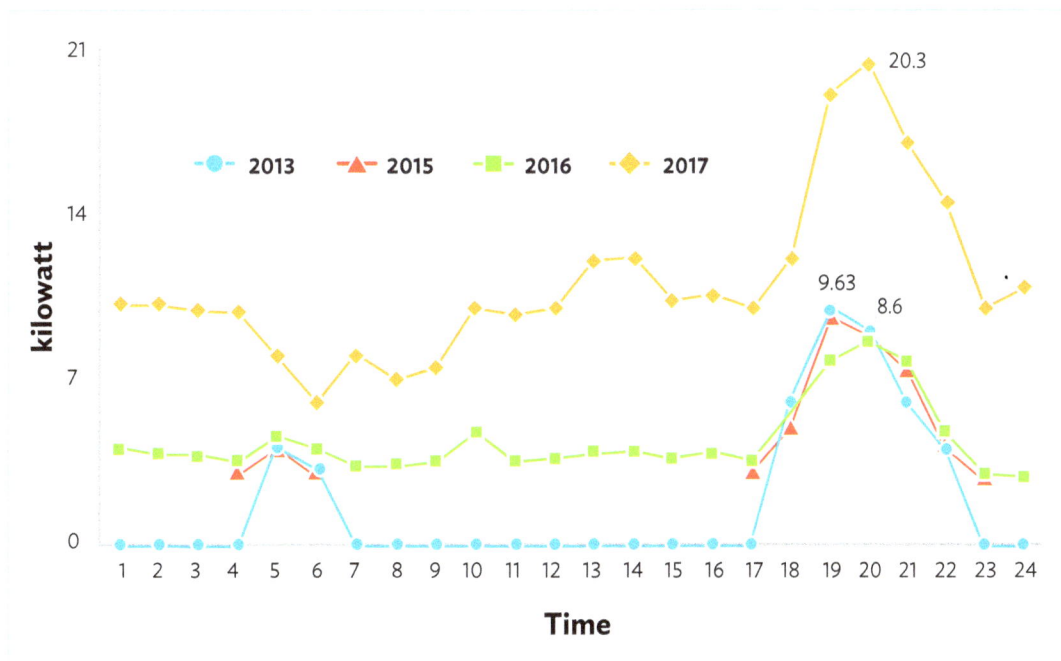

Source: Romblon Electric Cooperative.

6 Economic, Social, and Environmental Impact

Access to reliable energy generally fosters economic, social, and environmental benefits that lead to improvements in the quality of life of the local population. To verify whether these potential impacts were realized, a study that examined the improvements experienced by the beneficiaries of the solar PV–diesel hybrid project in Cobrador was conducted in November 2017. The findings are based on the results of interviews[14] and surveys of a random sample size of 56 households that represents 24% of the total population in Cobrador Island, and simulations of impact factors that only become apparent over time.

Greenhouse Gas Mitigation

HOMER was used to calculate the amount of greenhouse gas mitigated by the solar PV–diesel mini-grid hybrid system. The configuration of the pilot project can potentially reduce carbon dioxide emissions by 52,600 kilogram (kg) per year, compared to a business-as-usual configuration of diesel generation to supply the demand. Table 17 lists emission values that were calculated. The significant difference in emissions is clear between the two systems.

Table 17. Emissions Data for the Solar Hybrid System and the BAU System

Quantity	Solar PV-Hybrid System (kg/yr)	BAU Case: Diesel Generation (kg/yr)
Carbon Dioxide	6,179.00	58,803.00
Carbon Monoxide	15.30	145.00
Unburned Hydrocarbons	1.69	16.10
Particulate Matter	1.15	10.90
Sulfur Dioxide	12.40	118.00
Nitrogen Oxides	136.00	1,295.00

BAU = business-as-usual, kg/yr = kilogram per year.
Source: ADB.

---

[14] Interviews with key informants, among them, the barangay captain and members of the Barangay Council, school principal, day care center teacher, barangay health worker, midwife, and *sari-sari* (convenience) store operator were also conducted. The changes before and after the project are based on some recall and anecdotal evidence gathered during the survey while statistical information from ROMELCO are used to compare levels of consumption and tariff. Some concrete physical changes observed during a site visit are also used to illustrate and capture the impact of the project.

Impact on Access to Energy

Since 1995, ROMELCO has been generating and providing electricity to Cobrador residents using a 15-kW diesel generator. Service hours, however, were limited to 8 hours per day, due mainly to the high cost of diesel fuel which had to be regularly transported by boat from mainland Romblon. Per ROMELCO's billing information shown in Table 18, some 161 households, or 66%, were connected to ROMELCO's mini-grid system in 2015, with tariff rate pegged at ₱30 ($0.60) per kWh. (Although 170 households are known to be electrified, nine of the households are believed to access electricity by connecting to their neighbors.)

Table 18. ROMELCO Electricity Services from Hybrid Solar PV Power Generation

Item	2015	2016	2017
Households connected	161	190	260
Hours of service	8 hrs/day	24 hrs/day	24 hrs/day*
Electricity tariff	₱30/kWh	₱15/kWh	₱15/kWh

hrs = hours, kWh = kilowatt-hour, PV = photovoltaic, ROMELCO = Romblon Electric Cooperative.
*There was a period where the hours of service went down to 18 hrs/day as a result of the surging demand and extended rainy season when solar photovoltaic generation was low.
Source: ADB.

By 2017, (after the installation of the solar PV–diesel hybrid project in 2016), ROMELCO has connected 260 or 100% of households, including those that had earlier been receiving electricity through a neighbor's connection. In terms of coverage therefore, the project has provided universal access to electricity in the island. Aside from households served, ROMELCO has also connected community facilities, such as the barangay hall and health center, school, church, and has powered streetlights around the barangay.

Affordability

ROMELCO was able to reduce its electricity tariff by 50%, from ₱30/kWh ($0.60) to ₱15/kWh ($0.30) due to the partial displacement of the more expensive diesel fuel (Table 18). In addition, ROMELCO also extends discounts to lower-income households, i.e., 25% discount to those consuming up to 15 kWh and 20% discount to those consuming above 15 kWh up to 20 kWh per month. Majority of respondents (59%) found the tariff reasonable while 39% found the tariff still expensive compared to the lower price of electricity in mainland Romblon.

Impact on Households

Electricity consumption and expenditures. Consumption pattern by households in Figure 11 showed significant increases from 2015 to 2017. Electricity consumption by the average household tripled from an average of 8 kWh per month in 2015 to 24 kWh per month in 2016. This tapered down to 20 kWh in 2017 when the power plant experienced limited production. However, in the same year, some large residential loads were observed to have substantial consumption averaging 152 kWh per month. These were nonexistent in previous years and expected to appear only by 2021. Electricity usage by public service facilities likewise registered increasing trend from 24 kWh per month in 2015 to 25 kWh per month in 2016 and 29 kWh per month in 2017.

Translated into expenditures for electricity, consumers received more kWh of electricity for every peso they paid in 2016 and 2017, compared to 2015 (before the project) or conversely, they paid less for every kWh of electricity consumed. Table 19 shows the monthly consumption and expenditures of consumers in Cobrador from 2015 to 2017.

Working hours. With 24/7 electricity service, more electric appliances were being used. Appliances acquired by households after 2015 include electric fans, television sets, video compact discs, digital video discs, karaoke, radio, casette recorder, mobile phone, and rice cooker, among others. More light bulbs were also reportedly purchased and 5% of 56 households purchased a refrigerator or freezer (Table 20).

The availability of electricity throughout the night extended the working hours of households. Majority of the survey respondents (77%) reported using more hours for household chores, entertainment, and doing some agro-processing activities. Table 21 shows the number of households that increased their working hours and what these hours were used for.

Housewives engaged in more entrepreneurial activities, such as broom and/or basket making and other handicrafts while farmers were able to pack their goods for marketing the following day. Small store owners reported that they could now do repacking at night of sugar, salt, and other commodities that they sell at their stores. Adults and youth alike engage in more outdoor activities at night. Children can easily study and avoid straining their eyes studying by the light of kerosene lamps.

Livelihood and income generation. Survey results show that 16% of respondents experienced income increases in 2017 compared to 2015, 69% said their income remained the same, while 15% experienced reduction in income (Figure 12). This increase in income is confirmed in Table 22 where the reported monthly income profile shows a decrease in the percentage of households in the "below ₱3,000" income bracket from 47% in 2015 to 29% in 2017, and increases in the percentages of households in the "₱3,001–₱5,000" and "₱5,001–₱10,000" monthly income ranges. Moreover, there is also a slight increase in the number of households in the income "above ₱50,000" range.

Figure 11. Average Monthly Electricity Consumption in Cobrador Island, 2015–2017

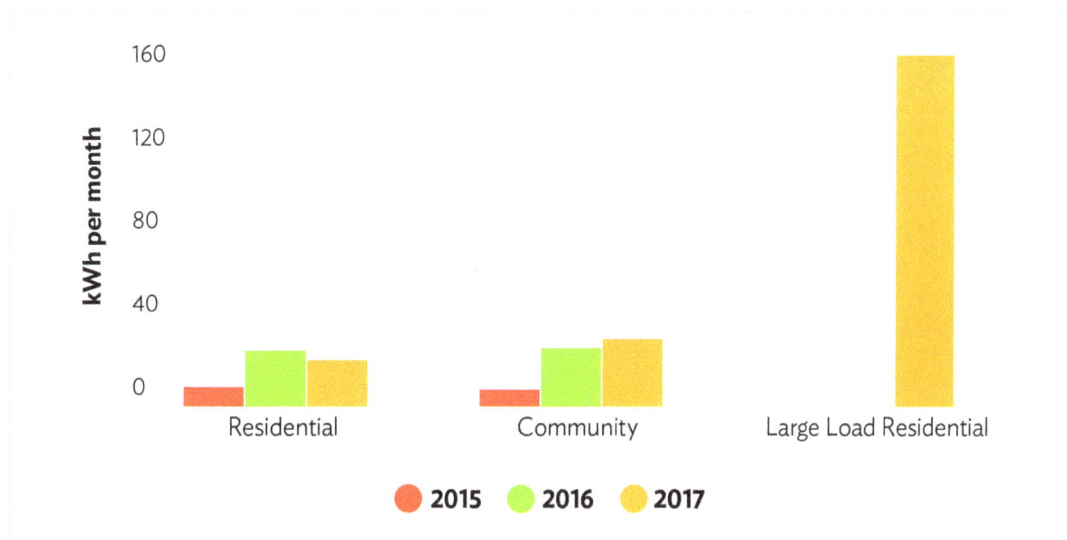

kWh = kilowatt-hour.
Source: ADB.

Table 19. Average Monthly Consumption and Expenditure, 2015–2017

Item	2015			2016			2017		
	HH	Large	Public	HH	Large	Public	HH	Large	Public
kWh Consumption	8	0	7	24	0	25	20	152	29
Amount paid (₱)	237		204	389		405	297	2,349	435
₱ price/kWh	30		29	16		16	15	15	15

HH= household or residential, kWh = kilowatt-hour, Large = household with large load.
Source: ADB.

Table 20. New Appliances Acquired

Type of Appliance	Number of Respondents	Percent of Respondents (%)
Electric fan	49	32.24
Television set	35	23.03
Video compact discs/Digital video discs	16	10.52
Light bulbs	13	8.55
Karaoke, Radio, Cassette recorder	11	7.24
Mobile phone	10	6.58

Continued on page 48.

Continued from page 47.

Type of Appliance	Number of Respondents	Percent of Respondents (%)
Rice cooker	8	5.26
Refrigerator, Freezer	7	4.60
Washing machine	1	0.66
Electric iron	1	0.66
Flashlight	1	0.66
Total number of new appliances	**152**	**100.00**

Source: ADB.

Table 21. Use of Extended Work Hours

Category	Number of Respondents	Percent of Respondents (%)
Housework	28	26
Entertainment	18	17
Agro-processing/animal breeding	17	16
Outdoor activities	16	15
Youth/children education	15	14
Small business	10	9
Barangay-related work	2	2
Total	**106**	**100**

Source: ADB.

Figure 12. Respondent and Household Perception in Change in Income

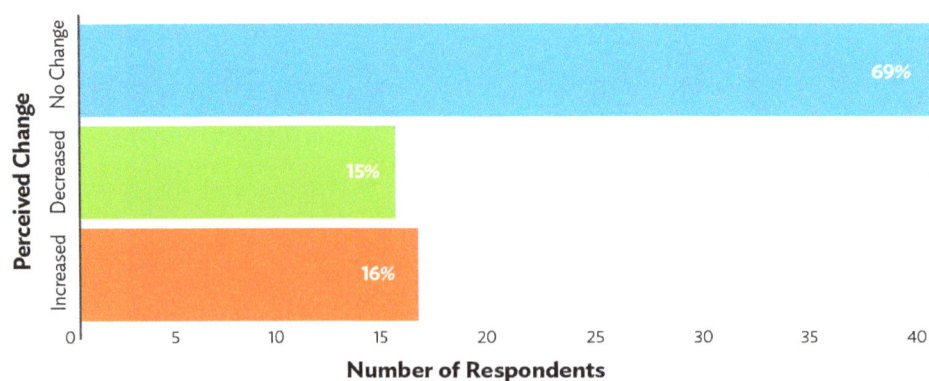

Source: ADB.

Table 22: Monthly Income Profile in Cobrador Island (Comparative 2015–2017)

Income Range (₱)	2015		2017	
	Number	Percent (%)	Number	Percent (%)
Below 3,000	26	47	16	29
3,001–5,000	7	13	15	27
5,001–10,000	8	15	12	22
10,001–15,000	1	2	1	2
15,001–30,000	4	5	1	2
30,001–50,000	2	4	2	4
Above 50,000	7	13	8	15

Source: ADB.

These survey results, when combined with some physical and anecdotal evidence, show that indeed some level of improvement in the economic status of residents have occurred because of the solar PV–diesel hybrid project.

New and enhanced livelihood opportunities in Cobrador Island came about mainly as expansion of stores, extension of store hours, and opening of new small stores, and from activities and businesses brought about by the increase in tourist arrivals. New stores often feature a refrigerator or freezer used for producing ice to support fishing activities and iced products for sale in the *sari-sari* or convenience stores. Fishers no longer have to go to the mainland to buy ice. With the freezers and refrigerators, they are now able to preserve their catch and sell these at higher prices. Housewives are also able to buy meat products and preserve them for later use. Some women have undertaken small-scale food businesses as they can now prepare food at night or at dawn for sale either at the school canteen or to tourist visitors. These women are beneficiaries of trainings conducted by the health center on cooking and safe food preparation.

With electricity, power tools and welding machines are now being used to ease carpentry and construction works. Fishers building their boats are benefiting from the use of these power tools. Entrepreneurial residents have also taken advantage of the availability of power by investing in new business opportunities. One resident operates an electricity-driven coconut grating machine. Another is building a new hostel with air-conditioned rooms for tourists.

Another positive development observed in the barangay is in-migration. Over the last year, some families have returned to the island. This is reflected in the higher number of household connections of 260 households reported by ROMELCO in 2017 compared to the 234 households count in 2015. Community organizations have been established and more shops have sprouted. Residents believe that positive social changes and opportunities in the barangay would keep the youth from migrating to the mainland or elsewhere in the country.

The availability of 24-hour electricity has also enhanced the tourism potential of the island. Cobrador has white sand beaches and pristine waters. Its location, just 40 minutes boat ride from the main island of Romblon makes it very attractive as a tourist destination. Some residents have taken on the task of serving as tourist guides. This positive development in Cobrador's local economy is also reflected in the barangay's increasing revenue trend, which posted a growth of 32% in 2017 compared to the barangay revenues recorded in 2015.

Impact on Community

Social services. The project generally brought same positive feeling and changes to the community. Observed changes include:

(i)   New infrastructure – Residents feel that their barangay is given importance. New infrastructures were built since the operation of the PV-diesel hybrid project. A covered basketball court was constructed beside the barangay hall, roads were improved, and streetlights installed. Plans are also underway for the construction of a water storage and delivery system.

(ii)   Improved barangay services – Delivery of social services generally improved. The barangay session hall installed air-conditioning for more comfortable meetings. At the day care center, children can watch movies, and sing and dance with a karaoke system. Children are also more comfortable indoors because of electric fans. The multipurpose hall can be used for community activities at night.

(iii) Secured community environment – Survey results point to a general satisfaction on the changes that have happened to Cobrador Island since the operation of the hybrid PV-diesel project. Ninety-eight percent of respondents said they like their barangay more than before. One main reason is the safety and security they feel now that the streets are well-lighted. Accidents are avoided and fishers can come home and land and anchor their boats safely even at night. The youth are able to enjoy clean, outdoor activities, such as basketball games in the evenings.

Health services. Improvement of health services is on top of the respondent's list of improved social services. With the availability of refrigerators for vaccines in the health clinic, health workers are now able to perform vaccination anytime. The health center can also provide better services, such as the use of nebulizer for asthma patients.

Barangay health workers feel less burdened in doing their tasks. There is convenience and efficiency in giving assistance to patients because of the lights, water dispenser, electric fans, air conditioner and appliances, especially during child delivery. They are also able to serve residents of the nearby community of Alad Island because Cobrador's health center is now duly recognized as a government maternity center. Childbirth can be performed any time of the day and night, and patients can now be confined in the health centers in case of emergencies.

The health center is also able to do more trainings on reproductive health, family planning, food processing, safe cooking, and cleanliness. Use of LCD projectors help facilitate and improve the training activities. There is likewise convenience in terms of report writing because this can be done at night.

Education. The availability of 24-hour electricity service has positively affected the way teachers carry out their profession. Electricity enabled the use of gadgets to enhance teaching methods and make learning more interesting. Thus, teachers were able to improve their teaching methods using modules from the internet, computers, LCD projectors, sound systems, and other audiovisual equipment. Classrooms are also more comfortable with the availability of lights and electric fans. The school's program has significantly improved with the use of multimedia equipment and hands-on computer classes, thus making it more conducive for learning and research. School attendance, student interest, and participation in classes improved because of the use of visual aids. The school has been able to hold school events and extracurricular activities even at night at the barangay's well-lighted multipurpose hall.

Environment. Eighty-one percent of respondents believe that the solar PV–diesel hybrid project has helped provide the barangay a cleaner environment. Because of the project, there is no need to use kerosene for lighting, resulting in less indoor air pollution. Children avoid exposure to smoke emitted by the kerosene lamps when they study at night. The use of diesel genset has been minimized, reducing both air and noise pollution.

The project has also made the community more environmentally conscious. A recycling initiative has been implemented as a result. With the influx of more tourists, the barangay is activating its Barangay Environment Council to ensure that the clean environment of Cobrador would be protected and preserved.

7 Conclusion

An enabling market and regulatory environment improves the financial viability of renewable energy hybrid mini-grids in isolated areas, which attracts private sector to rural electrification. Private companies will prioritize investing on sites with larger numbers of unelectrified households because demand will be greater. Government subsidies and incentives on rural electrification and renewable energy generation will enhance commercial viability of mini-grids where demand is low and operation expenses may be high. Conversely, countries with fossil fuel subsidies will expect slower adoption of renewable energy for rural electrification even in sites with abundant resources. However, operating expenses will surge once these subsidies are gone.

A geospatial map offers a basis for rural electrification planning. It provides a concrete and verifiable picture of a country's state of electrification. It can serve as an objective, apolitical rallying point for public and private sector actors who want to participate in national electrification. Clarifying the energy scenario at a township, city, or provincial level through geospatial mapping technology and reconciling this information with the aggregated capabilities and resources of participating actors can form the basis of a more realistic and robust electrification timeline.

This timeline can be used to gauge whether the pace of a country's electrification is sufficient to achieve their governments' local and international commitments on universal energy access. If the pace is below what is necessary, governments can then use the insight offered by geospatial mapping analysis to determine course of action.

Certain sites and areas could be too far from the grid, and electricity demand is not high enough to justify extending the grid. Mini-grid or distributed electrification can be explored for such cases, and this report has presented the Cobrador Island solar PV–diesel hybrid mini-grid. The Philippine government opted for a mini-grid in this island because expanding the grid using undersea cables was not economically viable given the estimated demand. Applying the methodology detailed in this report to the Cobrador case demonstrates that a diesel-solar PV-hybrid mini-grid is the least-cost electrification option.

Selecting the least-cost technology option is essential to make electricity affordable in isolated and remote mini-grids where households often have low income. Using available renewable energy resources will keep the operating expenses low. The HOMER simulation and optimization tool may be used to identify and design least-cost renewable energy and hybrid generation systems in mini-grids.

Outcomes of Applying the Methodology in the Philippines

The Solar PV–Diesel Hybrid Mini-Grid Project in Cobrador Island, described in Chapter 5, was initiated by the Philippine government to explore alternative electrification modalities for island communities. At the request of NEA, Energy for All analyzed the energy supply and demand characteristics of Cobrador Island and determined that hybridizing the existing diesel generator with solar PV is the least-cost option given the energy demand profile of the local village. The pilot project was successful because it demonstrated that

1.   ROMELCO, a distribution utility that had no prior experience with solar PV–diesel hybrid mini-grids, can develop the expertise to operate and maintain a sophisticated mini-grid system for an extended period.

2.   A solar PV–diesel hybrid mini-grid can provide Tier 5 electrification reliably to remote, off-grid communities.

3.   A solar PV–diesel hybrid mini-grid can achieve an operating expense-positive level of viability in the Philippines. A capital expenditure-positive level of viability can be achieved if the proponent is able to secure subsidy to capitalize its equipment—grants from ADB and KEA for the Corbrador case—or augment its electricity tariffs. Also, ROMELCO is a nonprofit EC, and ECs in the Philippines are assigned franchise areas where there could be losses at certain plants that could be offset from gains at other plants in their area.

4.   A relatively enabling regulatory environment supported the installation of the mini-grid. The government's rural electrification program through ECs, which are assigned franchise areas, has helped the Cobrador case. Aside from having sole license to operate in the area, ROMELCO, which has other plants in nearby islands, was able to consolidate efforts for O&M—staff who operate a nearby mini-hydropower plant provide O&M support to Cobrador's hydrid mini-grid.

A detailed account of the potential socioeconomic impact of the Cobrador mini-grid can be found in Chapter 6. While some of these depend on site-specific factors, the outcomes that are broadly applicable to sites that replicate the solar PV–diesel hybrid mini-grid are as follows:

1.   Greenhouse gas emissions from diesel generation is reduced.

2.   More reliable and abundant electricity encouraged households to replace kerosene lamps with LED lights. This, in turn, reduced the amount of indoor smoke and GHG emsisions at a household level.

3.   The delivery and quality of social services in a community improved. Interestingly, this impact affected migration patterns because locals are now encouraged to stay. A handful of families from nearby islands have also begun to move into Cobrador Island.

4.   More reliable and adequate access to electricity increased the level of economic activity in Cobrador Island. Access to medium-sized appliances, such as refrigerators and electro-mechanical equipment, increased the productivity and revenues of small stores and other microenterprises. Small resorts and inns have also sprouted along the island's white sand beaches.

5. The cost of electricity in Cobrador Island is now more resilient against the price fluctuations of petroleum because of the introduction of renewable source of electricity. Replicating Cobrador Island's solar PV–diesel hybrid in other remote islands and areas will contribute to the increased resilience of the Philippines' electricity costs against economic shocks.

Key Lessons from the Case Study

In the course of building, operating, and maintaining the Cobrador Island mini-grid, Energy for All encountered a number of issues that can be avoided in the future. Applying these lessons and insights in future iterations of the solar PV–diesel hybrid mini-grid can help strengthen sustainability and economic viability, and avoid unnecessary costs:

1. Subsidies and grants could play an important role in implementing a developing country's national electrification plan. ROMELCO would find it difficult to finance the subsidized portion of the Cobrador Island mini-grid, which is approximately $330,000 or 80% of the total project capitalization, using commercial loans or equity. Servicing such a loan, even with a low interest rate and reasonable tenor, would divert revenue away from overhead and other day-to-day operation and maintenance activities that are essential for sustainability. Equity investors will also find the dividend returns net of operating expenditures too low to be attractive. The capital expenditure subsidy from ADB and KEA, which the Philippine government facilitated, elevated the Cobrador Island mini-grid to an operating expense-positive business; the subsidy freed ROMELCO from amortization or dividend commitments, and has allowed it to fully allocate its revenues toward financing day-to-day operations. Since modern electricity services are public goods, the government will assist and initiate its provision.

2. Electricity consumption behavior is difficult to predict, particularly in areas where there is limited historical data. In the case of Cobrador Island, the abrupt increase in demand after installation—as locals purchased more and bigger electric appliances—placed a strain on the hybridized generation facility. This was only alleviated after ROMELCO increased the capacity of the system, which was a costly recourse because of the transportation of equipment and logistics arrangements for the additional construction in the remote island. This extra cost may be avoided with a combination of better demand estimates that anticipate the surge in electricity consumption after installation, and educating the locals with demand-side energy efficiency practices—such as promoting the use of efficient LCD screens, radio, electric fans, and other high-use appliances. Energy efficiency practices may also delay the need to increase generation capacity in the future.

3. It is also possible to overestimate demand, which could lead to underutilized assets and insufficient revenues to cover operation and maintenance costs. In such cases, the operator may stimulate demand by introducing productive end-use equipment and adjusting tariff rates to encourage more consumption. An affordable tariff rate is a strong driver of electricity consumption as experienced in Cobrador Island, where the tariff of the hybrid mini-grid was decreased by half, from ₱30 ($0.60) to ₱15 ($0.30) per kWh. While this rate is still higher compared to other areas within ROMELCO's franchise, the 50% drop in price encouraged more households to connect to the mini-grid. Households that were already connected also increased their consumption by acquiring additional appliances.

4. Building local capacity to operate and perform standard maintenance procedures is essential to sustainable mini-grid operations. In the case of the Cobrador Island mini-grid, the subcontractors hired by KEA to install, integrate, and operate the solar PV–diesel hybrid mini-grid trained ROMELCO's personnel to operate the system and perform routine maintenance procedures. Furthermore, the subcontractor installed a remote monitoring system to track asset performance and perform periodic diagnostic checks in real time. This combination of software and sensors minimized the risk of human error in day-to-day operations, and reduced the technical prerequisite to operate and manage the business. After the subcontractor completed the installation of the hybrid mini-grid, ROMELCO's personnel were given access to the remote monitoring system.

5. Dispatch strategies can be used to optimize resources and extend the life of the energy storage system. In the case of the Cobrador Island mini-grid, its system is designed to activate the diesel generator set during peak hours to prevent the battery from discharging at high current; otherwise, the battery's maximum storage capacity may drop prematurely. While this has trade-offs in fuel consumption and expenditure, the long-term gain in avoided battery replacement costs can be net positive.

References

Asian Development Bank, National Electrification Administration, and Korea Energy Agency. 2015. *Hybridizing Existing Diesel Power Plants with Renewable Energy: A Feasibility Study.* Unpublished.

M. Bhatia and N. Angelou. 2015. *Beyond Connections – Energy Access Redefined: Technical Report.* Energy Sector Management Assistance Program. Washington, DC: World Bank. http://documents.worldbank.org/curated/en/650971468180259602/Beyond-connections-energy-access-redefined-technical-report

International Energy Agency. 2017. *Energy Access Outlook 2017: From Poverty to Prosperity.* World Energy Outlook Special Report. Paris: IEA. https://www.iea.org/publications/freepublications/publication/WEO2017SpecialReport_EnergyAccessOutlook.pdf

———. 2018. *World Energy Outlook 2018.* Paris: IEA. https://doi.org/10.1787/weo-2018-en

T. Lambert, P. Gilman, and P. Lilienthal. 2006. Micropower System Modeling with HOMER. In F. A. Simoes. *Integration of Alternative Sources of Energy.* pp. 379–418. John Wiley & Sons, Inc.

National Power Corporation-Small Power Utilities Group. 2017. *Small Power Utilities Group: Power Plants and Power Barges Operational Report for Existing Areas.* 25 December. https://www.spug.ph/gridstat/Gridstat_122017_existing.pdf

Renewable Energy Policy Network for the 21st Century (REN 21). 2017. *Renewables 2017 Global Status Report.* Paris: REN21. http://www.ren21.net/wp-content/uploads/2017/06/17-8399_GSR_2017_Full_Report_0621_Opt.pdf

R. M. Shrestha and J. Acharya. 2015. *Sustainable Energy Access Planning: A Framework.* https://www.adb.org/sites/default/files/publication/160740/sustainable-energy-access-planning-fw.pdf

E. Terrado, A. Cabraal, and I. Mukherjee. 2008. *Designing Sustainable Off-grid Rural Electrification Projects – Principles and Practices.* http://documents.worldbank.org/curated/en/120391468313811877/Operational-guidance-for-World-Bank-Group-staff-designing-sustainable-off-grid-rural-electrification-projects-principles-and-practices

World Bank. 2017. *Regulatory Indicators for Sustainable Energy.* Washington, DC. http://rise.worldbank.org/indicators

www.ingramcontent.com/pod-product-compliance
Lightning Source LLC
Chambersburg PA
CBHW061225270326
41927CB00025B/3496